Donation from
# The Japan Forum
to the Department of
East Asian Languages
& Literatures
in celebration of
the 10th anniversary of
The Japan Forum.
1998

# DECLINE AND PROSPERITY

# DECLINE
# AND
# PROSPERITY:
## Corporate Innovation in Japan

Noboru Makino

KODANSHA INTERNATIONAL
Tokyo and New York

Distributed in the United States by Kodansha International/USA
Ltd., through Harper & Row, Publishers, Inc., 10 East 53rd
Street, New York, New York 10022. Published by Kodansha
International Ltd., 2-2, Otowa 1-chome, Bunkyo-ku, Tokyo
112 and Kodansha International/USA Ltd., 10 East 53rd Street,
New York, New York 10022. Originally published in Japanese
in 1985, under the title *Hanei to Suibo*, by Kodansha Ltd.
English translation copyright © 1987 by Kodansha International
Ltd. All rights reserved. Printed in Japan.
LCC 86-40434
ISBN 0-87011-810-2
ISBN 4-7700-1310-8 (in Japan)
First edition, 1987

# CONTENTS

# Preface

Not long ago, a film crew from West Germany's national television station came to interview me. Their first question was: West Germany has fallen behind the United States and Japan in high technology. Do you think that it will ever be able to catch up?

I replied, "When I first visited West Germany over twenty years ago and toured some of the leading plants in the country, my first impression was that Japan would never be able to catch up. Now that Japan has not only caught up but surpassed West Germany in many technological regions, I believe that West Germany, with its able workers, can do the same. However, there is one condition, and that is how seriously West Germany regards innovation."

Decline and prosperity are not choosy as regards the type of industry they affect. West Germany is a master of industrial technology, but it has lost its industrial vitality. In cameras, machine tools, automobiles—its traditional strengths—to computers, microelectronics and new technology, West Germany has been overtaken by Japan.

As for the United States, it is also showing signs of a lost vitality in industry, and as a result the economic friction between Japan and the United States is intensifying. Former Foreign Affairs

Minister Saburo Okita noted with alarm after a meeting with American officials in the summer of 1985 that Japan–U.S. relations seem similar to those on "the eve of a war."

In 1985 Japan rang up a record-breaking current account surplus totaling over $49.1 billion, and this is still growing as the visible trade balance—the largest part of the current account balance—is climbing to still higher peaks. And the United States, burdened with Federal as well as trade deficits, is understandably angry with Japan.

Yet the real reason for this anger lies not in the trade figures themselves but in the type of products that Japan is exporting. Until recently, such exports consisted mostly of TVs, textiles, and automobiles, but today they are photocopiers, machine tools—a voluntary export control item—and semiconductors, once the pride of American technology. With Japanese ultra large-scale integrated circuits now making inroads in the American marketplace, the United States' pride is hurt. It has lost face.

In another sensitive field, that of telecommunications equipment, the key to the coming information era, Japan is also recording large surpluses. This is also the case in computer-related equipment. As a result, in a few years time the only products that America can be proud of will be satellites and weaponry. At the same time, the United States is funding much of Japan's national security, while Japan's aid to developing countries is still mediocre. Considered in this light, America has every reason to be dissatisfied with Japan.

When we compare the industrial indexes of the major advanced countries, decline and prosperity are revealed in startling clarity. In the 1970s, the two oil crises served to halt the growth of the world economy, with some countries still in the throes of its aftereffects. However, in the case of Japan, it bounced back with great vigor, recording higher growth rates than other countries, with better current account balances, lower unemployment, and more favorable price indexes.

When a country prospers or declines, there is an accompanying prosperity or decline in its industry. Although industry as a whole is flourishing in Japan, an inside look reveals that not all companies share the same prospects. In short, corporations follow fixed patterns of "life expectancy." When I was looking for my first job, the three most sought-after companies were Mitsui Mining, Dai Nippon Spinning, and Daiei, the movie company. Today, all these companies have lost their former luster. Similarly, small subsidiaries have arisen from total obscurity to overtake their parent companies, e.g. Hitachi, the electronics conglomerate, once a small repair arm of Hitachi Mining. Or Fuji Photo Film—the second largest photo film producer after Kodak—which was once an inconsequential subsidiary of a manufacturer of celluloid products, which was, in turn, a trading company subsidiary. This goes to show that there is a generational change in the corporate world, and some companies are undoubtedly showing signs of aging.

This state of impermanence governs not only the traditional heavy and chemical industries but also the new high-tech and service industries. In all companies, decline and prosperity are but two sides of the same coin, whether viewed from an international standpoint or from within a corporation.

In this book I have attempted to analyze this decline-prosperity phenomenon. What are the factors that can strengthen an industry that is expected to decline? Why do some companies in declining industrial sectors still manage to flourish? The simple answer to these questions lies in innovation, and in this book the secret ingredients of innovation are sought through analyses of specific companies.

NOBORU MAKINO

*Tokyo, 1987*

# Changes Leading
# to Corporate Decline

The history of mankind is a history of change; yet at no other time has change played as great or as crucial a role in shaping our future as at the present. This transforming social environment is naturally reflected in the marketplace, where shifting consumer tastes and habits influence the types of goods produced. As the fight for corporate survival and prosperity gets tougher in the years ahead, what should corporations do in order to stay with the competition? How should they cope with these times of flux?

In order to answer this, we must first examine the factors that are altering the contemporary corporate climate. These can be grouped under six major headings. 1. Market saturation: our present society is marked by a surfeit of manufactured goods and a decline in basic industries. 2. The shift to an information society: the emerging importance of products that dispense information and their acceptance in daily life. 3. The advent of internationalization: the intensification of trade friction and the growing importance of newly industrialized countries (NICs). 4. Changes in demographic composition and the role of women: an aging population and the attendant changes in the structure and role of the family. 5. The expansion of the public sector:

mounting budget deficits, tax increases, and a growing reliance on private business. 6. The impact of high technology: the recurrence of a high-tech boom with a shift to software technology.

## MARKET SATURATION

Most businesses are concerned about the changes that will affect their market in the future, naturally enough since we all know that markets cannot expand indefinitely but will stop growing someday. The failure to take this into account in business strategy is a leading factor behind the downfall of many corporations. How long this takes is stated in the book *The Life Expectancy of Corporations* (published by *Nihon Keizai Shimbun*, 1984), which declares firmly that "the life expectancy of a company is thirty years."

Koji Kobayashi, chairman of NEC Corporation, put it in a similar way: "A business will expire in thirty years if it continues only to make the same products." And Takeshi Nagano, president of Mitsubishi Metal Corporation, says, "In my experience, no business can continue to flourish for over three decades."

A report published by the *Nikkei Business* magazine reviewed 413 top Japanese companies in terms of assets between the years 1896 and 1982. The number of companies that disappeared altogether in a single ten-year period numbered 194; those that vanished after three such periods totaled 309, which means that almost 80 percent of the 413 companies disappeared within a thirty-year period. It is safe to assume then that the life expectancy of an average company stands somewhere around twenty-five years.

In Japan the star performer in industry in the prewar and postwar era was coal, which managed to attract the best heads in the country, many of whom have become today's leaders in business and financial circles, such as Eishiro Saito, chairman of Keidanren (Japan Federation of Economic Organizations), and Bunpei Otsuki, former chairman of Nikkeiran (Japan Federation of Employers Associations).

Indeed the coal industry was regarded with much awe. I was told the following anecdote by Taichi Sakaiya, well-known author, critic, and a leading social commentator, about a friend of his who joined Toyota Motor Corp. after the war. Apprehensive of the future of the auto industry, the friend successfully applied for a job with Joban Tanko, the leading coal mining company then. When he told Toyota's personnel director that he had changed his mind about joining the company, he was immediately offered a raise if he stayed with Toyota. He declined, but perhaps later regretted his decision, for Joban Tanko ended up as Hawaiian Center, a hotspring hotel that has passed its heyday, while Toyota is now one of the world's leading enterprises.

Another example illustrating the ups and downs of corporations is shown by a study published in *Nikkei Business* dated January 22, 1985. It selected fifteen companies with a large number of Tokyo University graduates in their upper management—Tokyo University is the most prestigious in Japan, and its graduates can virtually pick which companies they wish to join. The study focused on the the correlation between the number of such graduates and the company's record of growth, and concluded that the greater the number of Tokyo University graduates in upper management, the slower the growth rate experienced in that company.

Companies like Furukawa (a major copper smelting firm belonging to the Furukawa group), Nippon Steel, Japan Air Lines, and Sumitomo Realty and Development, all of which had a high proportion of graduates from Tokyo University in upper management, saw a very slow growth rate. At the other end of the scale, a high growth rate was found in companies that had no graduates from Tokyo University, such as Hitachi Maxell, the magnetic tape and floppy disk manufacturer, Nintendo, which specializes in games, including electronic games, Royal, a suburban restaurant chain, and Secom, which markets private security systems. Companies that only had a few Tokyo University graduates in their employ also registered a high growth rate, such as Skylark, another suburban restaurant chain, Daikyo Kanko, dealer in condominiums, and Orient Leasing.

Despite the above, some data seemed to contradict the findings. For example, Tokyo Electric Power and Toa Nenryo, an oil-refining company with ties to Esso and Mobil, where 80 percent of upper-management members had graduated from Tokyo University, were found to have posted high growth rates. Later, however, it was discovered that this growth was only the result of a rise in oil prices. Finally, the only exception to the trend was Fanuc, the world's largest NC (numerical control) systems manufacturer, which had both a high percentage of Tokyo University graduates and a high growth rate.

I found this fact quite disconcerting as I myself graduated from the aforementioned university. However, the findings are not quite so surprising when you consider that in 1944, the year I graduated, it was relatively easy for a graduate with good grades to land a job with the top companies of the time—in the aircraft industry, in shipbuilding, coal mining, textile manufacturing, aluminum companies, and the cement, sugar, and fertilizer in-dustries, also known as the three "whites" in Japan. On average, new recruits would be around twenty-five years old, or thirty years away from upper management. If the life expectancy of a corporation is assumed to be under three decades, most of these businesses would be headed for a downswing by the time these recruits reached upper management age, and corporations with a large number of Tokyo University graduates would find themselves in a slow growth situation. So my advice to young people today is to find a job in a small company that has a sound management system, although I am not implying that all such small companies will eventually make it big.

The same situation is prevalent in the United States, where near-ly 40 percent of the 43 blue-chip companies analyzed in the book *In Search of Excellence* (Thomas J. Peters and Robert H. Water-man, Harper & Row, 1982) are now having problems. This goes to show how difficult it is for a business to survive and prosper.

Despite the ups and downs experienced by individual companies, the Japanese economy on the whole continues to grow. Some businessmen, however, looking at the surface of the present corporate climate, only see high growth prospects for companies in the electronics field. This is a much mistaken view, and my aim in this book is to correct it.

Japan's GNP today stands at approximately ¥300 trillion, and it has been growing at an average rate of 4 percent per annum for the past few years. If the nation's growth rate persists steadily in this fashion, the GNP will double to over ¥600 trillion in the next twenty years. Since it took Japan nearly three thousand years, from the dawn of its history, to reach the present figure, then the growth in the next two decades will be equal to that of three thousand years.

Thus what stands before us at the threshold of the twenty-first century is a market whose size is comparable to what the Japanese economy has achieved to date. However, in content, the new market will be totally different, and it is important to have a clear grasp of the changes that are going to take place in that market in order to keep ahead of the competition.

The one thing that is crystal clear is that growth in physical production has virtually come to a standstill. Comparing the situation today with that of 1945, Japan's economy has grown twenty times in real terms and fifteen times in per capita terms. Still, a person who used to eat five bowls of rice per day cannot consume seventy-five simply because the economy has grown that many times. And neither will the person who used to finish a bar of soap in three days manage any differently today, which is why one major soap manufacturer, Mitsuwa Sekken, went bankrupt.

Any market has a saturation point, and one of the clearest instances of this fact is the textile industry. When I was born in 1921, as many as twelve out of fifteen top businesses were in textiles. In 1929, the textile industry accounted for 44 percent of Japan's industrial output. Today, its share has dwindled to 4.8

percent, despite the fact that the economy has grown twenty times since 1929. People who used to own four or five suits in those days cannot afford eighty suits today; even if they could, they would not actually need more than ten.

The other day the chairman of Mitsui Real Estate Development, Hideo Edo, told me that in his opinion the housing industry had reached its peak. He remarked that ten years ago demand for new homes stood at 1.8 million, while today it is 1.1 million. "There's only one way to go now and it's down," he remarked sadly.

In Japan the total number of houses is 16 percent higher than the total number of households, and in this sense the housing market has achieved full growth as the demand for new homes has been fully met. New housing starts will drop to 900,000 a year, half of what it was ten years ago, but nevertheless it is too soon to be pessimistic about the industry's future.

While housing starts, or the commencement of construction of new homes, have declined, the number of houses that have already been completed has increased. This fact gradually revealed a whole new market in the construction industry, namely, that of house repairs, house renovations, rebuilding and additions, and house maintenance. The depressed housing market is estimated to total ¥1.3 trillion, but the market for renovations and maintenance is shortly expected to reach ¥10 trillion. Sales are still larger in new house construction, but the trend is sure to reverse. An interesting observation I made while at a meeting of the Federation of Specialty Stores Association in Japan, is that stores recording double-digit growth rates today are those that are primarily involved in the renovation business.

There is no future in the housing industry if we look at it through conventional eyes, but, from a service-oriented viewpoint, it has a brilliant future. Both Sekisui House and Mitsui Home, leading manufacturers of prefabricated houses, are operating profitably with their unitized, prefabricated products.

Both companies are providing services such as carpentry and plastering with their products. In this way the content of the housing industry, in keeping with the changing market, has evolved and changed.

The manufacturing industry consists of two separate industries: processing/assembling and materials. With the 1975 mining and manufacturing index standing at 100, the index for 1983 stood at 180 for the processing/assembling industry and 115 for the materials industry. What is the reason for this disparity? In the case of steel, which belongs to the materials category, demand is down because there is less need for products made from the metal. Even in steel-related industries, it is businesses that have some added value, such as engineering, and fine materials like ferrites (iron-oxide-related magnetic materials) that have prospects for growth. This kind of added value can be anything ranging from service to intelligence to emotional appeal.

Persevering in the same line of business without changing the content of that business spells decline and sure death; yet this does not imply that one should abandon one's main line of business. No businessman can switch to a completely new field of business overnight. He will need the support of his steady customers and his years of experience to make a success of it. In other words, an amateur is sure to lose if he takes on an expert. Of course, there are exceptional businessmen who are able to do this, men like Takami Takahashi, former president of Minebea, the world's top miniature bearing manufacturer, or the late Kenji Osano, chairman of Kokusai Kogyo, a conglomerate of over forty companies dealing in hotels, transportation, distribution, and banking among others, who until his death in 1986 was dubbed the last politico-entrepreneur.

However, to return to the discussion about abandoning one's main field in a business, there are always exceptions to the rule—companies that have successfully switched over to a completely new field. Take Kanebo, the former textile manufacturer, which changed to cosmetics, a bold step to say the least. However, from the point of view of Kanebo's clientele, who are mainly fashion-conscious women, the switch to cosmetics may not have been as drastic as first appears.

Some claim that Sumitomo Electric Industries and Sony have both strayed from their main line of business, the former by entering into fiber optics, and the latter by challenging camera manufacturers with its electronic Mavica camera. But the truth is that Sumitomo Electric, a manufacturer of electric cables, developed optical fibers in the course of finding a substitute for the copper used in its cables. Similarly, Sony's Mavica, a magnetic memory camera, is based on technology that is completely different from conventional cameras that record images by chemical changes. The Mavica is a VCR-related product, and represents a diversification of Sony's technical know-how in video recording devices, not an entry into the new field of camera manufacturing. Both companies, therefore, have changed the content of their main line of business with the aid of new technology. Similarly, the shift to service-oriented businesses, such as house renovations, suggests the path to new growth in the housing industry.

## THE SHIFT TO AN INFORMATION SOCIETY

First, what do the words "information society," mean? Let me attempt to explain them by examining three different areas: technology, merchandise, and labor.

Many products on the market today incorporate information technology such as integrated circuits (ICs): TVs, sewing machines, telephones, watches, and cameras. In May 1984, when the Ministry of International Trade and Industry (MITI) made public twenty items that recorded sharp growth from 1979 to 1984, all of them fell into the category of information-related equipment. The growth rate was 5.36 times for industrial robots, 5.33 for VCRs, and 4.56 for facsimile machines. Other items included quartz oscillators, metal oxide semiconductors (MOS), bipolar semiconductors, telephone systems, silicon rectifiers, ultra small motors, magnetic tapes, photoelectric conversion devices, computers, and diodes.

As regards merchandise, we can attempt a definition of the word "information" by quoting Tadao Umesao, the well-known social anthropologist and enthnologist. In a conversation with Hideki Yukawa, Nobel Prize–winner for physics in 1949, Umesao said that our world is made up of three things: material objects, energy, and information. If we pursue this train of thought, we can say that information is anything that is neither an object nor energy. In the industrial age, material things and energy took precedence over information; in the information society, it is information that is emphasized at the expense of the other two. In the production of merchandise, therefore, it is the value-added aspect in information technology that will become of paramount importance.

I mentioned earlier that the textile industry is declining. Yet Toray Industries is the leading manufacturer of synthetic fibers and was responsible for the development of carbon fibers, the material used in aircraft bodies, tennis rackets, and golf clubs. Carbon fibers are produced through the burning of acrylic fibers. Acrylic fibers cost around ¥800 a kilogram, but when they undergo the complex, technical process of being burned, their value shoots up to around ¥18,000 per kilogram. This added value is nothing more than intelligence, or know-how.

Toray's second best-selling merchandise is contact lenses. The spectacle market is worth some ¥300 billion today, or double that of industrial robots, and the sector especially worth watching is contact lenses. Toray concentrated on this field and developed a "soft" contact lens with a water content equal to 48 percent of its weight. Toray's president, Yoshikazu Ito, told me that each lens sells for between ¥30,000 and ¥60,000, but the material in the lens is only worth ¥15! Toray is not marketing the raw material but its R&D, or technical know-how, which can push up the value of the raw material two thousand times.

As regards labor, the following facts highlight the advent of the age of information. In 1960, the cost breakdown for a computer—the information equipment par excellence—was 80 percent for hardware and 20 percent for software. Twenty years later, the situation has reversed itself, clearly indicating that the need for jobs requiring brain power has risen faster than those needing production power. This fact is further supported by a look at the employee breakdown at NEC and Fujitsu, the computer manufacturers, where only 20 percent of personnel are engaged in physical production.

In the late fifties and early sixties, when I was with Mitsubishi Steel Manufacturing, I remember our shabby administrative office at the rolling mill and the hordes of workers in the plant, who all had a towel tied about their foreheads and wore leather-soled sandals, or *setta*, on their feet. Shoes could not be kicked off fast enough when sparks flew into them. Yet despite the precautions, accidents did happen. Not long ago, I had a chance to revisit that old workshop of mine, and I was astonished to see there was nobody on the factory floor at all. Instead, five or six bored-looking workers were sitting in the control room watching the computers that scanned the entire plant. The only staff remaining are those engaged in information-related jobs: software production, production control, marketing, design, and R&D. The situation is the same at Nippon Steel, the largest such manufacturer in Japan, and also in the manufacturing sector in general, where very few people are actually engaged in the production process.

The shift to an information society is apparent in changes in the composition of the work force, for such changes indicate which functions are gaining in importance today. The graph (*see* Fig. 1) shows those sectors of the American economy that have grown over the past twelve decades, from 1860 to 1980, in terms of the percentage of people working in them. The statistics are from the U.S. census, and although I have simplified it somewhat, this graph reveals social change very clearly.

In the case of Japan, the pattern traced by social change would be similar to that traced by the United States, but it would cover a shorter period of fifty years, from 1955 to 2005. Those polled were asked, "What type of work do you do?" not "What type of company do you work for?" Thus a steel company employee doing computer software work was not classified as doing industrial work.

The graph clearly shows the social changes that have occurred in the United States, almost half of whose working population was engaged in agriculture a century ago. The number today has declined drastically. The percentage of workers in manufacturing or in the industrial sector was just under 30 percent a century ago. It rose above the 30 percent mark, then declined to around 25 percent. In the service sector the work force has not changed much, so I left it out. But the greatest increase

Fig. 1: THE COMPOSITION OF THE AMERICAN WORK FORCE (1860–1980)

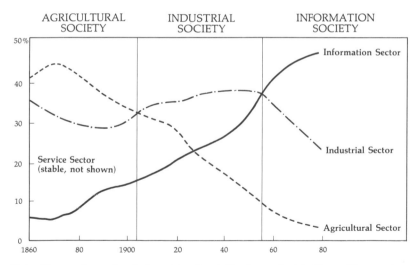

Note: The service sector, being virtually stable, is not depicted here. The number of people employed in the information sector in 1980 is an estimate.

has been in the information sector, from 7 percent in 1860 to 47 percent in 1980.

In order to gauge what is going to happen in Japan, match the year 1860 in the United States with the year 1955 in Japan, so 1980 in America would be 2005 in Japan. The patterns of social change trace the same curves on the graph. Those engaged in physical production are classified as belonging to the industrial sector, those in sales and general office work to the service industries, those in R&D, design, software, marketing, and production control to the information sector, and this is the sector that is growing rapidly.

If we label a society agricultural when the numbers engaged in agriculture form the majority, and a society industrial when those employed in production form the majority, then the year 1955 can be called an information society because it was then that the work force engaged in information became predominant.

In the United States, those engaged in manufacturing are called blue-collar workers, those in clerical work white-collared workers, and those working in the information industry gold-collar workers. These people are engaged in engineering, management, R&D, planning, and marketing, which make up the heart of the information society.

According to Robert E. Kelly's book, *The Golden Collar Worker* (published by Addison-Wesley, 1985), the unemployment rate in the United States for blue-collar workers is 16.7 percent, for white-collar workers 12 percent, and for gold-collar workers only 3.2 percent. This shows that people working in the information sector have greater stability of employment, and their number is growing.

## THE ADVENT OF INTERNATIONALIZATION

The third change affecting the business climate of today is the growing importance of internationalization. Japan is heavily dependent on overseas trade for its economic growth, and any adverse effect on the international trade sector will spell doom for the Japanese economy. Unfortunately, the international situation does not look favorable for Japan and the future of the Japanese economy is thus in jeopardy at the moment.

One reason for this is the growing volume of Japanese exports. Since 1945, Japan has concentrated doggedly on international trade until it now finds itself the second largest economic power in the free world. In 1985, Japan chalked up a $49.3 billion surplus in its current account balance, followed by West Germany with a $13.8 billion surplus, the United Kingdom with $5.3 billion, and France with $600 million. The United States, on the other hand, went the opposite way and registered a deficit of $117.8 billion.

However, when added up, these figures do not tally. The global current account balance has produced a continuous deficit of $100 billion for the past two or three years. These balance sheets should have some correspondence, just as in a game of mah-jongg: when someone wins a certain amount, another player loses by that amount. But in the case of world trade balances, the figures do not match up. Why?

Some say that this is due to "errors and omissions," for which the United States is largely responsible. There are three main factors behind the amounts attributable to such errors and omissions, namely, the armaments trade, underground money, and multinational corporations. The arms business is not listed in U.S. trade figures because it is regarded as a "service." Underground money represents the profits made from smuggled merchandise that cannot be openly marketed and these are not included in official statements. And the multinationals have their own ways of manipulating profits, not to mention the number of tax havens that exist for just such a purpose. Once, in a Diet meeting, an angry opposition member noted that only two of the Japanese trading conglomerates are paying any tax, which is outrageous. It is said that the multinationals even go so far as manipulating their purchasing prices after first calculating the country in which they are going to make their profit. Taking these three factors into account, the United States is not really in as bad a state as the figures seem to show.

Another example is Japan's overseas investment. Foreign securities and the like purchased by Japan amount to over ¥1 trillion a month. In 1984, such transactions totaled $70 billion. This money is pouring out of the country in the form of overseas assets, with the result that Japan now outranks the United States and the United Kingdom. Some countries criticize Japan for making double gains, once when selling the goods at a profit and then making that profit available as loans to foreign businesses. This is an area of mounting concern, for, despite the amounts Japan earns, it spends very little on defense or aid. While the United States spends ¥60 trillion annually on defense, an amount equal to the total cost of World War II, Japan's share is only an annual ¥3 trillion. It knows it can rely on the United States for its defense, and thus keeps such expenditure low. At the same time, Japan's official development assistance (ODA) is far below its economic capability.

Even though Japan's defense expenditure is a reflection of domestic public opinion, it is dangerous for Japan to continue to turn a deaf ear to its critics and to shirk its international obligations. Japan cannot get far without the support of the international community, and Japan's reluctance to spend more on defense and on international aid will have to be reconsidered for the sake of the country's future.

Another factor that is contributing considerably to world friction is Japan's large trade balance. Japanese exports are continuing to grow at an annual 42.7 percent (1984) and its trade surplus with the United States is rising commensurately. However, the issue with the United States lies not so much in the surplus as in the content of that surplus.

Today the trade friction between Japan and the United States centers around high technology. The U.S. Department of Commerce prepared a report entitled "Changes in Import Dependence on High-Tech Products of Major Countries," with high-tech products referring to those products in ten different fields that feature high growth and intensive R&D. The standard for high technology is calculated in terms of the ratio of the import of high-tech products to the export of high-tech products. When imports are equal in value to exports, the ratio stands at 100, while 40 will refer to the ratio of imports to exports standing at 100 to 40. Thus, the lower the ratio, the lower the imports and the higher the competitiveness of the country in the high-tech area. According to this configuration, Japan's figure for 1980 stood at 30, compared to 100 for France, 65 for West Germany, and 50 for the United States. Two decades ago, the figure was 20 for the United States, then the leader in the field. Today the positions of Japan and the United States have been switched.

In the mid-1960s, I made a tour of West Germany's AEG Telefunken and Siemens factories. They were indeed impressive, confirming my image of that country as the leading technological nation in the world. However, when I revisited the country in 1984, I learned that AEG Telefunken and Grundrich were both on the verge of bankruptcy, driven there by the influx of quality electrical appliances from Japan.

There was a time when Japan had to import all its high-tech wares from the United States, from communications equipment to computers to semiconductors. Today, Japan is ahead of the United States in automobiles and NC (numerical control) machine tools and, four years ago, started to compete in the semiconductor and communications equipment field. Japan enjoys a surplus in its trade in office automation equipment and computer peripherals. Thus, the source of trade friction between the two countries has shifted toward technologically sophisticated products. In a *Nihon Keizai Shimbun* poll of one thousand presidents of banks and corporations, in answer to the question, "How will economic friction develop with the United States and West Europe in the years ahead?" 60 percent answered that friction will be focused on the area of high technology.

How should Japan cope with this flood of criticism following its rise in stature in the world economy? Some gloomily say that Japan's fate is sealed and there is nothing to do but await ostracism by the world community, but I see three courses of action open.

The first is a relaxation of Japan's import restrictions, although I do not propose that this should be done across the board. In some industries, such as pharmaceuticals, further tests—beyond those already carried out in the United States and other advanced countries—on whether or not the medications meet Japanese standards should be abolished because they take so much time. Japan should rely on American standards as set out in the Action Program of 1985, which abolished a number of such restrictions. However, in the case of other imports such as machinery and manufactured products, U.S. specifications should not be accepted alone.

A relaxation of import restrictions may sometimes be complicated by differences in American and Japanese cultural traits and attitudes. In 1984, *Newsweek* magazine carried an article complaining about Japanese restrictions on American communications machinery. The reason for the outburst was that Japan had asked for information manuals in Japanese. Since the machinery is meant to be used by Japanese, it stands to reason that it should be in the language of that country. This is a case of Americans believing that their way of doing things is best and that their standards are, therefore, also better.

I was told by the top executive of an automobile company that when American auto parts makers visited his company to sell their products, the Japanese company had to hire an interpreter to talk with them. "That is ridiculous, don't you think?" he said.

When Japanese salesmen visit the United States, they make not only their manuals but also their products acceptable to American users. For the Japanese the customers are like gods, and one does not make demands of gods. But American salesmen often do, and faced with such unreasonableness, it is futile to relax our standards to meet with American approval. It is also quite horrifying to think that the Austrian wine scandal (where toxic antifreeze was added to wine) should occur in other sectors of the domestic market due to the indiscriminate lifting of import restrictions.

The second measure that Japan can take to cope with the growing trade friction is to set up manufacturing plants abroad. This step will serve the dual purpose of reducing the unemployment of the countries concerned and of pushing up their GNP. However, it is important that the R&D and design sections of the company should continue to be located in Japan.

Honda Motor Co. operates fifty-five motorcycle plants overseas. According to its director, Hiroyuki Yoshino, Honda's motorcycle division in Japan is in the red, but its overseas companies are flourishing. Why is this? The reason is that the motorcycle market in Japan is highly competitive, with major producers putting out new models with startling regularity. Honda's research lab in 1984 turned out fifty-two new models, while Harley-Davidson, the world-renowned American manufacturer, only produces one new model every ten years. This sort of competitiveness explains Honda's success in the United States.

The third course of action for Japan involves changing its economic policy, that is, expanding its domestic market. It is time for Japan to abandon its former policy of encouraging savings and to stimulate domestic demand both in consumer goods and in investment. In 1985, I had advocated that this move be coupled with an adjustment of America's high interest rates, a reduction of its deficits, and a rectification of the then high dollar exchange rate. These measures on America's part have all been achieved, and we are now left with the problem of the escalating yen rate vis-à-vis the dollar. Perhaps we should look at the situation in greater detail in order to determine what effects the rising yen will have on Japan's domestic market. Does a high yen have any positive results or will it be disadvantageous to both parties in the future?

If we set an average exchange rate for the yen in 1986 at 30 percent higher than the year before, what are the gains and losses for the country? If 30 percent of Japan's total exports, valued at ¥50 trillion, were lost because of the strong yen, the losses would amount to ¥15 trillion. Since two-thirds of Japan's export transactions is conducted in dollars, the final loss would amount to ¥10 trillion. Japan's imports for 1986 totaled ¥40 trillion, with only a small percentage being conducted in yen. Thirty percent of ¥40 trillion is ¥12 trillion. Subtracting ¥2 trillion for the part that is conducted in yen, we arrive at a gain of ¥10 trillion. Thus there is no loss and no gain on a national basis, assuming, of course, that the imports stay at the same level.

On a corporate scale, however, losses have been incurred, to the tune of ¥6 trillion, in overseas monetary deposits. A person who paid ¥2.4 million to buy $10,000 placed in an annual deposit would only receive ¥1.6 million back. It is said that insurance companies lost as much as ¥1.6 trillion in this way. Of course, those who borrowed from foreign banks have made gains, but they are very few in number.

More significant gains were made when the prices for oil and other primary products dropped. Lower prices for these commodities resulted in a ¥5 trillion gain in the case of oil and a ¥1 trillion gain for other primary products, totaling ¥6 trillion. Thus the loss of ¥6 trillion on overseas deposits is offset by such gains. However, the situation will not be so simple in the future, and it remains to be seen whether Japan can continue its export trade, with speculation and politics both having a significant effect on exchange rates.

I gained some interesting insights on a morning radio show in 1985, when I asked people in Europe and America about currency issues. For example, the way New Yorkers and people in Washington felt about the strong yen was very different. New Yorkers stressed economics and thought the dollar had fallen too far and should stay in the ¥170–180 range. Washingtonians, more politically conscious, said the reverse, that the yen should move still higher.

The yen–dollar exchange rate has entered the arena of politics, and only when the politicians reach an agreement will the rate be stabilized. Until Yasuhiro Nakasone's election victory in the summer of 1986, the dollar rate stood at the ¥160 level. Immediately after his reelection, it fell and stayed at the ¥150 level until the midterm U.S. elections were over. It is conceivable that the dollar will reach a much lower level in a year or so.

However, to determine the real exchange rate, one should take into consideration the following factors: commodity prices and trade and capital balances between the two countries. One should compare the economic fundamentals of the two—growth rate, world balance of payments, price stability, and unemployment rates—and this will reveal the relative strength of the two economies. When we do this we see that it is highly unlikely that Japan's economy will deteriorate suddenly in the next two or three years. Moreover, evaluating the two economies in terms of net overseas assets—of which Japan has the world's highest at $129.8 billion—only reveals a widening gap between the two. Therefore, Japan should devise an economic strategy based on the assumption of the dollar trading at ¥140.

The United States is forty times larger in area than Japan; yet the cost of the whole land area of Japan is higher than that for the whole of the United States. In the United States, gasoline costs under one-third its price in Japan, despite the drop in oil prices. Energy costs to operate a plant are also higher in Japan. And let us not forget that it was the high energy costs that drove the aluminum refining industry into collapse.

How can the manufacturing sector in Japan survive in view of all this, as well as the astronomical cost of labor? In 1983, when the yen was 30 percent lower, per capita GNP for Japan was $10,500 and $14,800 for the United States. At ¥160 to the dollar, Japan's per capita income will be higher than that of the United States, and at ¥157 to the dollar, it will rise above that of Switzerland's to become the highest in the world. It is hard to believe that Japan could become the highest income earner in per capita terms, for nothing has changed particularly in a year's time. If the cost of living was to go down in relation to the rise in the value of the yen, things would be fine, but in the past year, wholesale prices have gone down 10 percent and consumer prices have held steady.

When I was in Paris last year, I went to the Tour d'Argent for their famous duck dinner. With wine and escargots, the bill came to about ¥18,000. The same dinner at its restaurant in the New Otani Hotel in Tokyo cost me ¥30,000, and there were only five thin slices of duck for the main course. Before complaining to the manager, my friends told me that three slices of duck went toward the cost of the land and the chandeliers. The Paris restaurant, in existence since the fifteenth century, must have lower overheads than the restaurant in Japan, which has just started.

For businesses, the situation is a very serious one, since higher wages will inevitably push up product prices. Toyota Motor Corp., for example, has 60,000 employees, and the employees of companies under its umbrella number a further 300,000–400,000 people. A cut in wages without a cut in the cost of living is impossible to foresee. The effect of high wages will be reflected in the prices of exports, resulting in a grim future for trade. If the exports of the large corporations fall, the smaller companies dependent on them will surely be affected. This is a very serious problem indeed, and one that needs immediate attention.

## CHANGES IN DEMOGRAPHIC COMPOSITION AND THE ROLE OF WOMEN

The fourth change affecting the business climate today is Japan's graying population, resulting in the declining vitality of personnel in responsible positions in the business sector. In the consumer sector, there is a change in personal tastes and spending, which accounts for nearly 60 percent of the GNP. And in the fiscal sector, there is a growth in pensions and an increase in medical bills. Thus, the study of changes in demographic composition is crucial to any business that is attempting innovation.

The greatest change in population is the marked increase in the number of senior citizens, aged sixty-five and over, which stood at 9.9 percent of total population in 1984. However, by the year 2000, it will have risen to 20 percent, with the projection that by the year 2020, Japan will have the highest percentage of senior citizens in the world.

The influences of this graying society on the economy is diverse. First, there is an overall loss of vitality that is the natural outcome of any society that has a high proportion of aged citizens. Second, an increase in older members of society will mean a shortage of managerial positions in business. According to data produced by Mitsubishi Research Institute, graduate employees over the age of fifty in managerial posts now account for one-third of total employees. Supposing that the number of managerial positions stays constant, in ten years time the number of employees lucky enough to be in such positions will be one-third of the total, with the remaining two-thirds relegated to join the "window-seat tribe," so called because they are promoted and thus get to sit by a window but have no responsibilities at all. This problem is further exacerbated by the rise in the mandatory retirement age, so employees in their forties today will see the same bosses in their midst when they reach fifty. There is a joke going around that says that future design of office buildings should have as many windows as possible.

The third influence of the graying society is seen in increased pension payments. By the year 2000, one in five Japanese will be aged sixty-five or over. Let us assume, for the sake of simplicity, that half the population will be working by then. It means that every 2.5 people will have to support one elderly citizen. As the pension of an employee who retires at the mandatory retirement age of sixty amounts to 60 percent of his former salary, this means that every worker will have to contribute nearly 30 percent of his salary for the retired worker. This is far too much and can only result in a sort of "war" between young and old. Just as in the past, when the workers fought the employer for a share of the profits, in the future we will see the young pitted against the elderly. It remains to be seen whether the outcome in Japan will be the same as in other countries with high taxes, for example, Sweden, where there is a steady migration of workers into countries with lower taxes.

Graphically presented, the composition of the Japanese population is barrel-shaped, with the bulge representing those born in the first baby boom between 1947 and 1949. This is followed by a second bulge, representing the children of this generation, who, as leaders in consumption, culture, and politics, exert a profound influence on the economy.

Marketing targeted for this group can bring in huge profits for certain businesses. Wacoal, for example, the leading manufacturer of ladies underwear, brought out its shape-up panties, or girdle-panties, five years ago, and these proved to be an instant hit with over 3 million panties sold. Wacoal aimed its product carefully at women of the first baby boom, who are now at the age when they begin to worry about their figures. The shape-up panties are based on the "independent suspension" concept used in cars, according to a company spokesman. Furthermore, they are well designed and come in sixteen colors.

"Pay attention to the women entering their forties," advises Kimindo Kusaka, managing director of Softnomics Center, a software producer. In a popular TV quiz show on NHK, the public radio and television station, the panel was asked the question, "Seventy percent of middle-aged housewives in Japan have a job. True or false?" The answer, amazingly enough, is true. Or, more accurately, the figure of working wives stands at 66 percent. In addition to the excellent pay their husbands bring home, these women work to be able to afford the luxury of spending money on themselves.

What are these housewives like and how are they different from housewives in other countries? First, Japanese wives are not only rich but are also powerful, since it is they who hold the purse-strings, unlike in most countries where it is the husbands who control spending. Japanese husbands usually receive a monthly allowance from their wives.

Second, Japan is a country where most people finish high schools and where the proportion of those who go on to college is high. Thus, Japanese women are also very well educated, with 95 percent of them college or university graduates, compared to 75 percent in the United States and 30 percent in West Germany. Furthermore, the population density in the cities also has an effect on lifestyle. With the plenitude of weekly and monthly publications, as well as the seven television channels in Tokyo, the women are exceptionally well read and well informed.

Third, since women aged forty comprise the largest sector of the population, and since the Japanese are easily influenced by trends, these women are trend-setters, influencing younger wives in their spending habits.

Fourth, because of the availability of part-time jobs in this country, these women possess a great deal of confidence: if they get divorced they know they can find a job anytime.

Fifth, these housewives have a lot of time on their hands. With their children at school and plenty of electrical appliances to take care of domestic chores, they have free time and want to do something apart from housework, judging from the number of home-delivered lunches I saw outside the doors of an apartment block in a TV program.

However, one fact impressed me greatly about American women: the number of women in managerial positions. On a tour of the United States to inspect new media, I was greeted at AT&T by five managers, two of whom were women. At another company there was a woman vice president. In Japan women very rarely make it to manager, though it is certain that women will make greater advances from now on in various fields.

This change in the role of women has had a big impact on Japanese society. In the United States (*see* Fig. 2), the number of families in which the man worked and the woman stayed at home was 43 percent in 1960, 25 percent in 1975, and is projected

## Fig. 2: FAMILY COMPOSITION OF AMERICAN WORKERS

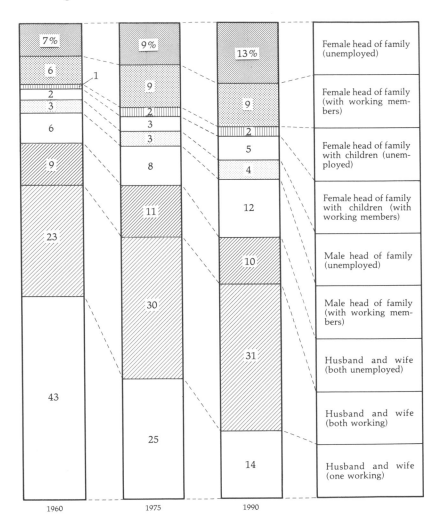

Source: *The Nation's Families* (National Livelihood Indexes,
Economic Planning Agency, 1985).

to decline to 14 percent in 1990. Conversely, families where both husbands and wives worked was 23 percent in 1960 and will rise to 31 percent in 1990. Nonworking single women families will rise to 13 percent in the same year. Families relying entirely on welfare is also expected to reach 10 percent in 1990. It is only a question of time before Japan's family structure changes in the same way, and thus the Japanese should prepare themselves for such an event.

Accompanying the change in the role of women was the role played by supermarkets to bring about a new distribution system in Japan. Through such innovative attempts as self-service, computerized management, and direct purchasing bypassing wholesalers, some supermarket chains have managed to increase sales one-thousand-fold in a matter of a few years. Masatoshi Ito, president of Ito-Yokado, one such chain, confided in me five or six years ago that sales stood at ¥1 billion twenty years ago, then jumped to ¥30 billion ten years ago, and now exceed ¥1 trillion. Another success story is Daiei, run by Isao Nakauchi, a former drugstore owner, who has managed to build, in two to three decades, an enterprise with annual sales topping ¥1 trillion. These two firms show how much can be accomplished through business innovation.

The flourishing supermarket business is a direct result of the increase in the number of working women. In the past, by the time these women came home from work, most of the neighborhood stores were shut, and the situation thus resulted in the now-ubiquitous "convenience stores" that stay open until midnight or later and have over two thousand goods in stock. Seven–Eleven Japan operates under an "umbrella" system, where some forty stores are located in an area that is easily covered by one truck supplying fresh products and food in one or two hours. This allows them to stock several thousand kinds of merchandise without ever running out of stock. These stores have all been born out of necessity through changes in family life, which will continue in the years ahead. Corporations cannot afford not to try and "preempt" such changes through business innovation.

## THE EXPANSION OF THE PUBLIC SECTOR

This, the fifth change in the business climate, is often referred to as the "developed nation's disease," whereby an expansion of the public sector goes hand-in-hand with a decline in industry, as seen in the United Kingdom. Although the problem is usually discussed from a macroeconomic viewpoint, its relation to the operation of businesses cannot be discounted. Just where the public sector is headed is a problem that affects all corporations.

"The developed nation's disease is here to stay," said Ryuzo Sejima, special adviser to C. Itoh & Co. and a member of the government's Special Advisory Committee on Administrative Reform, in a newspaper article. The disease can be summarized as follows: with the danger of a growing deficit in state finances, the government transfers part of the burden onto the people. This burden comes in the form of higher taxes, more social security payments, more health insurance and pension contributions. With larger payments, people will soon begin to think it is easier living on welfare than finding a job, an attitude that affects a country's vitality by sapping the people's vitality. Worse still, as the country's welfare system improves and expands, taxes and social security payments increase accordingly.

The situation is readily visible in those European countries that are in the throes of the disease. In recent statistics, tax and social security payments expressed as a percentage of income amounted to 60 percent for France, 52 percent for West Germany, and 30 percent for Japan. The low figure for Japan indicates that there is room for expansion in the future. Characteristically, the countries with this disease have a larger annual expenditure expressed as a percentage of GNP.

Illustrated in Figure 3 are changes in the ratio of annual expenditure in relation to GDP (gross domestic product). Two factors emerge quite clearly. The first is that Japan has increased its ratio of annual expenditure to GDP quite rapidly over the past ten years. This situation is due largely to the government's "wasteful distribution" of welfare money and the big increases in public spending before and after the oil crises of the seventies. It is evident that Japan is slowly but surely headed for the developed nation's disease. The other factor that can be gleaned from the chart is the Japanese abhorrence for any tax increases despite the low amount they have to pay.

Assuming that we do not increase taxation, how is the country to restructure its finances? I think that the only choice it has is to return to the level of fiscal spending of ten years ago. This method has been put forward by the Ad Hoc Commission on Administrative Reform. There is little hope of success for the government's present method of fiscal restructuring by holding the budget below a set ceiling. This will only make it necessary to institute indirect taxes or abolish the tax exemption on savings.

Fig. 3: GENERAL NATIONAL EXPENDITURE (as ratio of GNP)

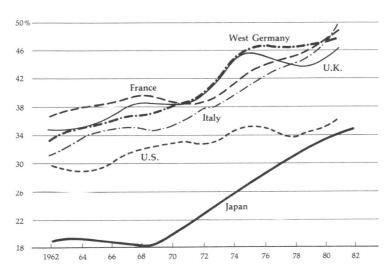

However, a reform of the present administrative structure through the elimination of wasteful public operations is timely, for only through taking this step can reform be brought about. The recent privatization of former public corporations such as Nippon Telegraph and Telephone (NTT) and Japan Tobacco Inc., as well as the division of the Japanese National Railways into six private companies, is one method for reforming inefficient public corporations. It can be described as "the culture of private sector vitality," where private sector vigor is injected into the public sector through a deregulation of government controls and funding.

Just how inefficient are Japan's public corporations? A report put out in late 1984 by the Local Government and Economic Society made a comparison of how much it would cost private companies and government offices to do the same job. For garbage collection, for instance, private companies estimated expenses at ¥6,630 against the government's ¥14,521; school lunches prepared by part-time women cost ¥64.56 per student against ¥114.93 when made by government workers. A janitor at a school cost ¥4,407,000 a year in salary, while a part-time employee could do the same job for ¥1,261,000.

The above data refer to average cost differences to run a city with a population of one hundred thousand. Being more goal-oriented, private companies will also provide better customer service and cost less. A look at some new service businesses, where growth is especially high, will reveal how important service and cost are to growth. These businesses are all in the "agency" sector, such as the Securities Patrol Agency Co., CSK Co., a computer operating service agency, and Recruit Co., which provides recruitment services.

Japan's cumbersome government services can definitely be trimmed to pave the way for fiscal restructuring. Streamlining these services, together with abandoning subsidies to public corporations, will result in cutbacks in fiscal spending. Public works investment has declined of late, and plant and equipment investment is also being cut back, but these measures will encourage their own set of problems in the form of a further stagnation of domestic demand. Japan, under fire from foreign countries over trade friction, can no longer depend on expanding external demand. However, if both domestic and foreign demand is reduced, the economy will be in a very serious condition.

The only saving grace is the huge amount of savings in the country. Japanese savings, totaling ¥460 trillion, were once loaned by banks to private businesses in need of funds for plant and equipment investment. However, private sector spending has declined since the two oil crises, and spending in the public sector is affected by cutbacks in fiscal expenditure. On the personal horizon, consumer spending is low because most people are saddled with housing loans and higher educational expenses.

The Japanese are, by nature, savers. They do not like to spend even though they have money in the bank. This is flowing out of the country in the form of overseas investment to the tune of ¥1 trillion a month. Japan is awash with cash and does not know what to do with it. A long time ago, when I was director of the Ichikawa plant of Mitsubishi Steel Manufacturing, I had to beg for a loan from the bank's section chief, who looked at me haughtily while I made repeated bows. Today, the situation is exactly the reverse. My son, who works in the loans section of a bank, has to peddle all over town on a bicycle to find prospective clients.

With plant and equipment investment at a low ebb, public works spending leveling off, and personal consumption in the doldrums, the Japanese economy has to be in serious straits. Up to now it has been in good health due mainly to its exports, which made up for the slack demand at home. Exports are far higher than imports both in manufactured goods and money, a factor for which Japan was taken to task at the Bonn Summit in 1985. With strong foreign criticism, however, it is unlikely that Japan will keep on increasing its exports. Indeed, the trade situation is so fraught with tension that one journalist likened it to "the eve before a war." With a decline in export volume, on which Japan is so dependent for economic growth, both its economy and its industries will be toned down considerably.

To avoid such tension with other countries, Japan has to increase its domestic demand. A tax cut on private capital spending will stimulate plant and equipment investment; and people will have to be encouraged to spend their savings to stimulate consumer spending. One conspicuous difference between Japan and the United States is that Japan gives preferential treatment to savings at the expense of investment, whereas the situation is exactly the opposite in the United States. Today, 60 percent to 70 percent of savings is tax-exempt, with most savers paying no tax at all.

Public works programs, now in a stage of retrenchment, should be encouraged to become a fundamental pillar for fiscal restructuring in the long term. The country's infrastructure needs improvement and expansion, and this will become more evident as the years pass. Today 60 percent of cars have to pass through Tokyo in order to reach other cities, towns, or villages, making the city even more congested and adding to the time lost. This loss has been calculated to run around ¥2 trillion per year. Should the government plan to construct two bypasses, one to the Tokyo Bay Coastal Road, and the other to the Central Connection Road (the loop road with a radius of fifty kilometers), the cost of construction over ten years is expected to amount to ¥2 trillion.

The effects of such construction was calculated in the following way by Genpachiro Konno, professor emeritus of Tokyo University. Suppose that the investment in road construction is increased at an annual rate of 6.8 percent. This will yield the aggregate value of ¥30 trillion: ¥12 trillion will be for direct benefits such as the shorter time needed to reach the destination; ¥18 trillion for indirect benefits. The construction will run up to ¥12 trillion calculated until the year 2000. In other words, an investment of ¥12 trillion will yield ¥30 trillion.

It is not enough for Paul Volcker, former chairman of the U.S.

Federal Reserve Board, to ask Japan to expand domestic demand. We ourselves have to urge for the "cultivation of private sector vitality" through the relaxation of various government regulations, administrative reform, and other means.

## THE IMPACT OF HIGH TECHNOLOGY

The sixth and last factor affecting the business environment of today is the impact of high technology. Breakthroughs are occurring with ever-increasing frequency as barriers are crossed annually. All these developments are closely followed by the mass media, and this is the ideal time to sow seeds in preparation for the advent of the next century.

It is perhaps worth relating the history of Japan's involvement with technology since the end of World War II. Japan's technological development had been characterized by three phases, the first covering the two decades after the war until the 1960s. This period is typified by "imported technologies" from Europe and the United States in all areas of the manufacturing industry, from televisions, transistors, and computers to rockets, jet engines, nuclear energy, ferrites, ductile cast iron, polyester, antibiotics, and so on. Almost no technology was developed by Japan.

In those days American and European manufacturing plants were willing to teach us whatever we wanted to know. As far as technology was concerned, we were a third-rate country, which dispatched engineers in droves to study foreign manufacturing processes. We were shown everything we wanted to see, and we took advantage of this kindness by stealthily taking measurements of the new machines we were shown and even bringing some machines home. Today, engineers from Europe visiting a magnet factory where I once worked are doing exactly the same. However, those Japanese companies that successfully incorporated imported technology into their manufacturing plants are all leaders in their fields today.

The second phase of Japan's involvement in technology coincided with its period of high economic growth in the 1960s, after having assimilated and mastered the foreign technology. Top priority, in terms of technology, was placed on the manufacturing industry in an effort to maximize productivity. Steel mills, chemical plants, and others competed vigorously in their economies of scale to try and increase productivity.

Let me first clarify what economies of scale mean. Suppose you have a glass filled with water. If you double the height and diameter of the glass, the surface area of the glass will be quadrupled, while its capacity will be increased eight times. So if you wish to treble the capacity of a blast furnace from one thousand cubic meters to three thousand cubic meters, all you have to do is increase the surface area of the furnace 1.7 times. In financial terms this means that you will have to spend 1.7 times as much money in order to treble output.

From the 1960s, Japanese companies continued to enlarge and increase the production capacities of their plants until colossal dimensions were reached. Where once a six-hundred-cubic-meter blast furnace was sufficient, it was expanded to two thousand cubic meters, then doubled, reaching five thousand and eight hundred cubic meters today. These economies of scale prevailed in every sector of Japanese industry. An average ethylene plant now produces two hundred thousand tons, while a power station that used to generate one hundred thousand kilowatts now produces one million kilowatts. Expand, expand, and expand characterized this phase of technological development in Japan.

This preoccupation with size led to two new currents, one of which was the Japanese development of technology. A movement calling for Japan to produce its own technology arose from the humiliation of always having to turn to America and Europe for guidance. This trend gained momentum and paved the way for Japan's successful entry into the field of technology. In a Gell-Mann Research Institute report, commissioned by the National Science Foundation, a country-by-country comparison was made in five hundred breakthrough technologies developed since the war. Japan, with no technology of its own until the 1960s, rated zero, while the United States, with the largest number, rated 60 percent. In the 1970s, the United States again held the top position, albeit with a lower percentage, followed by the United Kingdom, with, surprisingly, Japan in third place. Japan, with no important technology produced in the 1960s surpassed West Germany, the leader of the developed nations in Europe, France, and Canada in the 1970s. That was a great day for us engineers.

Accompanying Japan's entry into technological development in the 1970s, a second current occurred, namely, the beginnings of industrial pollution, the negative side of the coin of economies of scale. Newspapers of the time were filled with articles playing the same tune, that technology was evil, and factory managers appeared on television, their heads bowed low to apologize to antipollution activists. And we engineers felt very small indeed. Improved productivity, aided by the policy of economies of scale and expanded production technology, had yielded adverse secondary results, putting the brakes on the progress of technology.

We learned a lesson that economies of scale, pursued relentlessly, will result in a concentration of industrial wastes, thereby causing pollution. From then on, Japanese industries changed course and turned their efforts toward the development of pollution-controlling technologies and, in my opinion, the engineers did a superb job. Several years ago I made a visit to the Ogimachi plant of Nippon Kokan Corporation, Japan's second-largest steel manufacturer, and found green-colored equipment all over the place. These were antipollution devices attached to converters, blast furnaces, and coking ovens. In fact, green equipment predominated over black, or production, equipment, indicating the emphasis placed on pollution control in the plant. There was also hardly any smoke emitted.

A week later I visited a plant of Tissen in West Germany, the largest steel manufacturer in Europe, which brought to mind an old PR film on Yawata Steel, the predecessor of Nippon Steel. The film was entitled *The Rainbow in Our Skies*, and showed smoke rising from the plant over Yawata City in seven different colors, which it lyrically compared to the colors of the rainbow. This was the scene I saw at Tissen, with yellow smoke billowing here and purple smoke there.

The diligence and earnestness with which Japanese industry tackled the pollution problem is exemplified by the automobile industry. Once the question of toxic carbons emitted from car engines was taken up in the Diet, the auto industry became the butt of criticism everywhere, with the result that today it is only Japanese cars that can pass the Japanese tests for carbon monoxide emission controls. Antipollution research had unexpectedly led to improved engine performance in Japanese cars, with the pollution problem resulting in improved technical skill.

The third phase of Japan's technological development came into being in the 1980s, with a host of new technologies. In electronics, there are new functional devices, very large-scale integrated circuits (VLSI), optical fiber communications, and optoelectronics; in power and energy, we have fast breeder reactors, nuclear fusion, fuel cells, and solar cells; in materials, there are amorphous metals, superconductive materials, whiskers, and structural ceramics; in chemistry, there are various reagents, gene recombination, and functional polymers; and in machinery, we have mechatronics, robots, space shuttles, and linear motorcars.

Whenever we talk of technical innovation, we are apt to think of it only in terms of the manufacturing sector, which is a mistake. Japan's manufacturing processes have an overwhelming advantage over those of other countries in the world. In terms of productivity, if the index for Japan stands at 100, the United States is 93, West Germany 75, and the United Kingdom 45. Up until now high technology was limited to the manufacturing sector, but from now on the transfer of that technology into other fields is urgently necessary. This "transfer technology" is a characteristic of the present decade, and its application can be seen in the fields of banking and distribution, where electronics has entirely revolutionalized the procedures.

If we envisage the manufacturing industry, incorporating the best of high technology, as a fifty-story highrise, then the service industry can be likened to a shabby, ramshackle hut standing at the foot of the building. It is a fact that in the service sector Japan lags far behind: if the Japanese index stands at 100, the United States is ahead at 178. This is the area that Japan has to tackle in order to bridge that gap.

However, the mere existence of this large gap is not entirely a disadvantage for Japan. An analogy can be found in a team of golfers with a thirty-six handicap player in its midst. Spurred on by his betters, the handicapper may one day reduce his handicap to ten. This will never happen if the whole team consists of handicapped players.

It is in the service area that Japan should concentrate on in the age of technological innovation. High technology such as new media, and computers, and management technologies such as the "just-in-time" systems should be transferred to the service sector, for instance, in supermarkets, publishing, and transportation.

# 2

# Conditions for Corporate Survival

When we see how competitive the business environment really is, management according to conventional methods cannot even insure survival, let alone prosperity. The only way to avoid the inevitable decline that will affect most businesses in time is to instigate innovation. However, the word "innovation" is usually associated with technological innovation, which is only part of the solution, for technological innovation by itself is too narrow to enable you to move with the times. A wider implication of the word should be encouraged, more in the order of Professor Joseph Schumpeter's definition of innovation in the sense of "managerial innovation," or "corporate innovation," aimed toward growth in the future. This is more in character with the leading businesses of today.

## CORPORATE INNOVATION

Innovation conducive to future growth can be subdivided into three types: organizational innovation, product innovation, and technological innovation. Organizational innovation is achieved by streamlining the structure of the company or by reorganizing the distribution system, best illustrated by Ito-Yokado, McDonald's Japan, and Yamato Transport, the door-to-door parcel delivery service. Product innovation involves the manufacture of goods that are adapted to changes in consumer spending, such as Wacoal's fashion underwear for older women, Secom's private security systems, Ajinomoto's precooked foods, and Yakult's health drinks. Lastly, technological innovation involves growth based on the development of new technology as well as on the reorganization of the production system, such as Sony's VCRs, Sharp's pocket calculators, Casio's digital quartz watches, Nippon Steel's continuous casting, and Kikkoman's biotechnology.

Without taking any of these innovation measures, it is very unlikely for a business to survive for over three decades. Yet there are two exceptions to the rule: two companies listed in the Japanese stock exchange have been growing steadily in sales and in profits for the past two decades, both of which belong to the "printing" trade. They are Dai Nippon Printing and Toppan Printing.

I have used quotes around the word "printing" in order to emphasize that the printing they do differs enormously from conventional printing. In the case of Dai Nippon, sales from the printing of books and periodicals account for only one-fifth of total sales, with the remaining four-fifths coming from printed objects for commercial use and printed paper products. Dai Nippon is also involved in printing on various materials, ranging from iron sheets and format paper for computers to pattern transfers on building materials. Using its advanced plate-making technology, the company also manufactures masking screens for color TVs and photo masks for the transfer of circuit patterns on semiconductor substrates. In fact, there is no aspect of printing that Dai Nippon is not involved in, and in its operations it uses all available printing technologies to the utmost. The same holds true for Toppan Printing.

The greater part of their operations do not signify a break from conventional printing but rather an "expansion" of the printing industry. In other words, these two companies have significantly expanded on the usual sphere of work covered by the printing trade and, with the decline in the publishing business, are turning to new fields. That is the secret of their continuing success, and it shows us how important it is to expand our principal business when initiating any kind of innovation.

The second important factor to keep in mind in any innovation is the consumer. At Toppan Printing, staff responsible for the development of new technology are very conscious that innovation should be attempted with the view to developing merchandise that meets consumers' needs.

Dai Nippon employees talk about "creating orders," quite the reverse of ordinary printing companies that only act on receipt of an order from a client. Dai Nippon employees are motivated to "create" their own orders, meaning that they themselves have to think of new ideas that will generate public demand.

A product that is not in demand will not sell, no matter how excellent it is. What sells is what appeals to the consumer, and any innovations made will have to correspond to consumer tastes. This attitude is of vital importance when instigating any such measures, and necessitates keeping your antennae switched on to catch any shifts or trends in consumer needs. Only after this is done should you carry out your innovation, bearing in mind not to depart from your main line of business but to expand it.

*Organizational Innovation*

The basis of any innovation is organizational innovation, which is the first step in implementing any type of innovation. There are two approaches to organizational innovation: internal innovation within the company, and innovation from outside.

Let me embark on the discussion of internal organizational innovation with a few examples. Some companies manage to flourish even though they are in a declining industry. In 1985, I met two striking men who have succeeded in rehabilitating companies in such ailing industries. One is Hisao Tsubouchi, nicknamed the "king of Shikoku," who has diverse business interests ranging from shipbuilding, tourism, and newspapers on the island of Shikoku. He has amassed a huge fortune and is a powerful personality.

Mr. Tsubouchi was present at a management seminar where I had a chance to talk to him. He told me that Sasebo Heavy Industries Co. had accumulated losses of over ¥100 billion when he was asked to take on the job of rehabilitating it. That was after Japan's major shipbuilding companies had all tried to salvage the company, each for a period of two to three years. In the end these companies only managed to add losses of ¥20 billion to ¥30 billion.

When they finally gave up, Mr. Tsubouchi stepped in and, within a few years, managed to clear the deficit, turning a profit of several million yen. How did he do it?

Mr. Tsubouchi's secret weapon was internal reorganization. Sasebo Heavy Industries had over four hundred personnel in managerial positions, which Mr. Tsubouchi cut down to thirty-eight. Despite this drastic reduction, production increased, showing up the inefficiency of the previous management. I asked whether he lost a lot of capable people in the process, and he replied: "My policy of having a few good managers rather than a large number of mediocre ones means that those who retained their positions after the cutbacks became the 'select few.' "

The rehabilitation of Sasebo Heavy Industries was accomplished by resorting to a series of strict financial measures, some bordering on the unnecessary, as the following episode reveals. Rumor has it that when the nuclear-powered ship *Mutsu* docked at Sasebo port for repairs, Mr. Tsubouchi built a fence around the dockyard and collected an entrance fee from the repairmen sent by the manufacturer of the nuclear reactor.

Still it is a fact that drastic and thorough streamlining, and internal reorganization, put this deficit-ridden company back on its feet. And no one was better qualified for this than Mr. Tsubouchi, who is well known for his bold approach to the work force. I chanced to meet him again two to three months after he undertook the rehabilitation of another ailing company, Hakodate Dockyard, by first cutting back one-third of its work force. However, he claimed that he never had to fire a single employee. He explained: "I own some three hundred companies, including taxi companies, movie houses, and golf links. Since the companies that need my help also only need two-thirds of their work force, I send the superfluous workers to my other companies. Only in cases when they refuse to relocate do I have to resort to firing them."

Men who are good at this sort of work often have similar facial features, and the second striking personality I met was Umeo Ohyama, president of Tsugami, a major machine tool manufacturer, famous for his knack of reviving ailing companies. He showed me a leather pouch he was carrying that contained the official seals of the thirty companies he had charge of (such seals are usually kept in a locked safe). He then said that no expenses totaling over ¥100 were allowed unless he affixed the seal on the payment slip. The statement drew a groan from me. Even a jam bun costs ¥70 today, and Mr. Ohyama controls expenses in hundred of yen! When he talked about cutting down on expenses, he means it literally, it seemed. What is clear is that neither of these men deal in half-measures, which end in failure, but carry their resolutions through to the utmost.

Another point that these two men agree on is that managers of failing firms often tend to mix their private expenses with company expenses. Some managers charge their bar bills or other personal gifts to the company and, in the most extreme case, one manager even built a house at company expense. With such men at the helm, no company will be able to show a profit; moreover, morale will be low and accounting chaotic, certain to lead to bankruptcy in the long run. Yet neither Mr. Tsubouchi nor Mr. Ohyama are born misers who hate to part with money. The former shares his profits among his employees and the local communities where his companies are located; Mr. Ohyama contributes all but his salary to the Ohyama Foundation, which he established for the purpose of medical research. Both men have succeeded because of their uncompromising attitude to organizational innovation, the key to managerial innovation in the years to come.

However, internal reorganization alone, without the accompaniment of external streamlining, is not sufficient. By external organization, I mean the innovation of the distribution system, which is noticeably backward in Japan.

When asked to name the most inefficient enterprise in Japan, no one hesitated to say the former Japanese National Railways (JNR), which had accumulated losses of over ¥1 trillion. In normal circumstances such a company would have gone bankrupt long ago. However, having been an adviser to JNR's Management Planning Office some years ago, I am familiar with both the good and bad points of this organization.

Two reasons can be cited for JNR's huge deficit. The first is the number of politically built lines in existence, pledged by politicians in order to win support from voters. These lines are little used and represent an extremely wasteful operation, with the JNR forking out ¥1,000 for every ¥100 earned. The second reason for JNR's deficit is its freight division, which is severely in the red. Over twenty years ago, this service handled over 50 percent of the nation's freight. What happened? The answer is that JNR failed to make innovations in this sector.

The passenger division made innovations by inaugurating the Shinkansen "bullet train" service in 1964 that enables one to make a same-day business trip from Tokyo to Osaka and vice-versa. This trip used to take seven hours one-way. The Shinkansen revolutionized passenger transportation, yielding recurring profits that account for about 40 percent of sales.

The freight division, on the other hand, did nothing at all and was operating exactly as it had been for decades. For instance, your uncle in Niigata Prefecture sends you some quality rice by JNR freight. You wait a few days and nothing arrives, so you go to the nearest station to inquire about it. The clerk there has no idea where the parcel is. In other words, there is no information about the whereabouts of the package or its estimated time of arrival. This was no different from the situation at the beginning of this century, so naturally people eventually stopped using the service.

Instead, they turned to the trucking services that carry packages by road. Once you entrust a package to such a company, it knows where the truck with your package is minute by minute. The newer door-to-door parcel delivery services are also proving very popular with customers. When my wife went to Shikoku six years ago, she bought some fresh fish produce famous in the region and sent it by door-to-door delivery service. She was a bit worried that it might spoil if it did not arrive quickly, but it was on our doorstep the evening after she returned to Tokyo. In addition to the speed of transportation, the companies charge a reasonable ¥800 for every ten kilograms. I thought these prices might spell ruin for the companies, but Yamato Transport, the largest delivery company, reported a profit of ¥40 billion six years ago. Today it handles over 100 million parcels annually, far more than the post office.

The biggest factor contributing to the soaring growth of these door-to-door delivery companies is their "information management." Every parcel carries a bar code that is read by a sales office computer and the information is fed into the host computer. This network covers the entire country, and the information on each parcel is controlled by the VAN (value-added network) system of communications.

This online computer network laid the groundwork for quick, sophisticated, and low-cost delivery services, resulting in the revolutionization of the nation's freight system. This network, furthermore, managed to transform that most backward of service industries called distribution, which, in turn, had a tremendous effect on marketing. Marketing underwent a revolution through the introduction of a new distribution concept, that of distribution "trading houses." This system reduced the loading and unloading three times to a single time. Evident in major cities today are the large stores dealing in cameras, watches, televisions, VCRs, and CDs for 30 percent to 40 percent below their list prices. Yodobashi Camera and Doi are two well-known names. The reason they are so successful lies in their streamlined distribution system.

For example, if a consumer durable carries a price tag of ¥100,000, then roughly ¥40,000 is the ex-factory product price and the remainder is distribution costs. The retailer, the last in a series of distribution stages, then adds a 25 percent margin to the retail price, resulting in the price of the product climbing from ¥40,000 to ¥100,000. Furthermore, all these different stages means a delay of six weeks before the product reaches the consumer. Similarly, it was brought to light in a recent campaign to buy imported goods that the price of a bottle of whiskey imported for ¥800 soared to almost ¥10,000 by the time it reaches the consumer due to the various taxes and middlemen. It is thus possible to greatly reduce prices if goods are sold directly to the consumer, bypassing the distribution stages in between. Nor will there be inventory worries, since orders will arrive quickly, without the delay incurred by middlemen. A streamlined distribution system only means benefits all around.

In addition to these new distribution "trading houses," Seino Transportation, a leading firm in its field, has plans to station about 50,000 "echo ladies" throughout the country. These ladies, mostly middle-aged women, will make door-to-door visits in their respective zones to collect orders for cameras, televisions, furniture, and other goods explained in a full-color catalog. The merchandise will then be delivered by door-to-door parcel service in two or three days, thereby eliminating what would otherwise be a six-week delay. The only expenses incurred are the wages for the women. In this way, the distribution company performs the functions of a trading company, making full use of the VAN communications network. This is an innovation—a departure from conventional retailing methods—and although the plan is still on the drawing board, it promises to force a reform on the whole marketing system.

Even companies that are not involved in distribution have reaped the benefits of success through direct contact with consumers. One such company is Hoya, the crystal, glassware, and spectacle frame manufacturers. Headed by Tetsuo Suzuki, Hoya's sales are rocketing up despite the difficulties it experienced in the first two to three years after establishing a direct sales system. Such difficulties were no more than a natural outcome of the overhauling of the previous system.

Another successful company that is benefiting from a direct sales system is Kao, the manufacturer of soaps and detergents and women's sanitary products. The added advantage of a direct sales system is that, in addition to streamlining the distribution system, the company is able to build an outstanding customer service system because it places the manufacturer directly in touch with consumer needs. This is of supreme importance in the development of any new merchandise. Kao has set up an around-the-clock service to monitor all inquiries, and it is said that a department chief is there to take calls from customers even at midnight. In other words, the company is listening to the opinions of its customers directly.

*Product Innovation*

With the growing pace of changes in the marketplace, no innovation of any significance can be accomplished without first grasping what the new consumer needs are.

A diversification of interests in consumer behavior today brings with it an entirely new type of market. Ten or more years ago, for instance, only twenty-four kinds of beer were available in Japan, and they all came in large bottles. At that time beer was the drink at most formal social events, where people made toasts with glasses of beer. Today over two hundred types of beer are available, and they come in big, medium, and small bottles, in cans of different sizes, and in barrels. Women have also joined the beer-drinking ranks, and they are showing a preference for canned beer, even going so far as to say it tastes better. Younger men, on the other hand, prefer draft beer in barrels.

This trend toward diversification can be observed in a whole range of manufactured goods, and the automobile serves as a perfect example. In the past the car that was the automaker's yard-stick was Ford's Model T, the mass-produced car that came only in black and had identical interiors. Today the situation has changed beyond all recognition. When I toured Toyota Motor's Takaoka plant, the managing director told me that the plant produced only Corollas, but that they came in thirty thousand different types.

In 1984, I toured the Wolfsburg plant of Volkswagen, where the Golf models are made. These cars come in three hundred thousand types, depending upon customer specifications regarding color, type of steering wheel, wheels, and seats. And they were all being assembled on two conveyor belts. How can two belts manage this? The secret lies in the computerized production system. On the identical steel chassis of each car is a bar code that has the programmed information of the customer's specifications, and this information is fed into a computer. The pre-ordered parts are read by the computer and supplied to the relevant section of the assembly line. The workers merely have to assemble the parts of each car according to the program on the computer.

The use of the computer in factory production has enabled a wide range of diversified goods to be produced on a conveyor belt. In recent years, these flexible manufacturing systems (FMS) have increased in number and are able to produce goods tailored to smaller, more specialized segments of the market.

The spending habits of people have changed dramatically in recent years. Today a lot of young people ride motorcycles or scooters, among them a number of girls, who seem to get a great kick out of being watched. When these youngsters purchase a motorcycle, they are not buying the tangible object but the "intangible" object: part of their enjoyment stems from riding a motorcycle in fashionable gear. They have made the merchandise a tool of sensual pleasure and "performance," in this case of their self-expression.

When you are attempting product innovation, it is important to know what the consumer needs and what kind of "sensual" pleasure he is seeking. The following story about Mazda, the automaker based in Hiroshima and in Kyushu, illustrates the point perfectly. Ten or more years ago, Mazda was in a serious situation, with its factories full of unsold cars and production at a standstill. The company as a last resort decided to send all its employees on a massive research mission to find out what the consumers wanted. Mazda's former president, Yoshiki Yamasaki, remarked that when the employees left Hiroshima Station, "it was like seeing off soldiers going to the war."

However, the effort paid off in the long run. Mazda's staff in the manufacturing, planning, technological, and administrative divisions scoured the country to find out what type of car consumers wanted, and when they returned they incorporated these results in the Familia, a new model that sold like hotcakes when it first appeared.

Another aspect of manufacturing hitherto neglected but proving to be more important is service. The service industry as a tertiary industry has grown remarkably, but as yet untapped is the "service" embodied in manufactured goods. For those who think that service is confined to restaurants and supermarkets, let me list the sort of services that can be provided by the manufacturing industry.

1. **Maintenance service.**  Computer software, for instance, accounts for 80 percent of the total cost of information processing. Of that figure, 60 percent is for maintenance. The figure is the same for factories, robots, cars, and houses. In the car industry, the number of plant workers totals two hundred thousand, while the number of garage mechanics totals three hundred and twenty thousand. Similarly, more profit comes from the maintenance of gas boilers than from their sales.

**2. Service in food products.**     If Ajinomoto had produced nothing but the monosodium glutamate seasoning used in Oriental cooking, it would have gone bankrupt long ago. Its diversification into precooked and instant foods struck a responsive chord in the housewives of today, many of whom are working women. When these women return home after work, the last thing they want to do is spend thirty minutes preparing the miso soup that accompanies every Japanese meal. Instead, they use the instant miso soup that is ready in seconds. The instant soup may cost three times more than the home-made variety, but that cost is already made up for in time and energy saved. This explains the popularity of convenience stores with take-out foods and fast-food outlets, such as McDonald's.

**3. Labor service.**     House repairs and maintenance constitute a growing market these days, and available today are unit houses and unit bathrooms that are selling well because they are offered together with building-related services such as carpentry, plastering, and scaffolding.

**4. Business service.**     This is exemplified by automatic vending machines, machines that punch tickets at railway stations, automatic warehouses, and office automation equipment. All these businesses are expected to record large growths in the future.

In conclusion, how has consumerism in Japan changed? For a start it is clear that the "have" era is now past, for Japan is a materially affluent nation, unlike thirty years ago when all Japanese wanted to own such tangible things as houses, TVs, or cars. The present age is very much a "do" age, with people wanting to go on overseas trips, attend cultural classes, or learn some handicraft. In the next generation Japan will enter a "be" age, when people will enjoy doing nothing other than being where they are. The young girls at my institute are now going abroad and spending a week at a Spanish seaside resort rather than dashing around Europe seeing the sights. And the time will come when Japanese will take a full hour over their lunch rather than wolfing down noodles in fifteen minutes. However, with the coming of the "be" age, I see a decline in the vitality of Japanese industry, an inevitable accompaniment of the "be" society.

## Technological Innovation

In the types of innovation mentioned above a crucial role is played by technology, and the recent boom in high technology will bring with it possibilities of growth in several sectors.

After graduating, I was about to join my first company, Nippon Kokan, which was then involved in the production of iron ingots. When I suggested to a senior engineer that we develop a magnetic material, he laughed and said, "Look, ours is a large company with over one hundred thousand employees. Tokyo Denki Kagaku Kogyo, which specializes in magnetic materials, only has one hundred men. Why should we join that market?" The situation after forty years shows that the big five steelmakers in fiscal 1983 had a combined deficit of ¥50 billion for the first half of the year, while Tokyo Denki Kagaku Kogyo, now renamed TDK Corp., posted a profit of ¥50 billion for the same period. Who's laughing now?

This shows how technological innovation can yield colossal gains. Magnetic materials belong to the same category as iron; yet it was their development that was responsible for this large gap in company performance today. If only the steelmakers were bold enough to digress from their main field and pay attention to a growth product such as magnetic materials that, in function, are similar to iron, their business position would be far more comfortable now.

A parallel situation exists in the cement industry, which was very big after the war, with the presidents of cement companies holding the top positions in the country's economic organizations. Today all these companies are in a state of decline. However, the situation is just the reverse in the field of new ceramics, which belongs to the same cement industry. Kyocera, founded by eight people twenty-eight years ago, is now an enterprise worth an annual ¥65 billion and employs over ten thousand workers. This huge advance is accounted for solely by the development of new technology, in this case new ceramics.

Industries that continue to grow and expand all share a common trait, that is, they do not stop developing new technology or coming up with new products. Take Matsushita Electric Industrial Co., more familiarly known as National in Japan and Panasonic in the United States, which is constantly bringing out one new product after another: refrigerators, color TVs, VCRs, compact discs, laser discs. While watching the "life expectancy" of one product, it comes up with the next one, and so on. Furthermore, National's products have always kept within the household electric appliance field.

Such companies are able to expand with technology developed in-house and increase the range of their products. The Seiko group started out with clocks and watches, then brought out electronic watches, and is now making printers. By keeping a watchful eye on market trends, Seiko catered to consumer needs, which enabled it to expand in new market directions. Thus technological innovation does not mean branching out into a completely different market just because such a market looks promising. One must also take great care not to make mistakes when diversifying.

With all the different types of new technology in existence that can contribute to the growth of business, it is natural to feel a bit confused as to which one to choose. The foresight and skill of engineers is put severely to the test today, and it may be simpler if we begin by dividing new technology into hardware and software.

## HARDWARE TECHNOLOGY

1. **The integrated circuit.** The IC is the basis of the computer, and advance in computer technology is only possible through advances in IC technology. The computer forms the core of the information society and as such is closely related to telecommunications, with the one multiplying the effects of the other.

Computers have made spectacular progress since the development of the large-scale integrated (LSI) circuit, and particularly noteworthy is the advance in microcomputers. Therefore, the field where growth is most remarkable is IC technology.

**2. Optotechnology.**    The use of optotechnology has expanded into several fields with the development of the laser, ranging from telecommunications, processing, measuring devices, to medical diagnosis, and the computer. Lasers, with their short wavelength and energy concentration, are a good example of optotechnology.

**3. Telecommunications technology.**    Also called "new media" in Japan, this technology is expected to play a leading role in the first half of the 1990s. New media such as CATV (cable TV) and CAPTAIN (character and pattern telephone access information network), satellite communications, character multiplex broadcasting, and optical fiber communications are advancing rapidly, and information network systems (INS) that coordinate these new media will come into more general use.

**4. New materials technology.**    New materials with electronic, magnetic, optical, and biocompatible functions are becoming the nucleus of this technology. Other new materials include amorphous metals and functional resins.

**5. Biotechnology.**    In our "biosociety" the impact of biotechnology that is capable of imitating living organisms is far-reaching. Breakthroughs in gene recombinant technology is attracting world attention, and the development of biomechanics and biosensors will expand application of this technology into production of industrial robots, artificial hearts, and so forth. Today, companies are betting heavily on this field becoming the next core technology.

Other new technologies that are expected to gather importance in the next century are biotechnology, space technology, and new energy technology.

SOFTWARE TECHNOLOGY

Software technology, or "intangible technology," involves programming, artificial intelligence, operation research, simulation, and the Delphi projection method has seen strong advances in recent years.

**1. Computer software.** The market for this software technology has been expanding vigorously and is worth ¥1.3 trillion today, compared to the ¥1 trillion market for computer hardware. Furthermore, since software is crucial to the manufacture and sales of the computer, and most computer hardware companies are also involved in some measure in the production of software, this field is even larger when such factors are taken into account.

**2. Intellectual technology.** The success of artificial satellite projects lies not in the progress of machines or electronics technology but in the systems management that integrated these advances. Making full use of a variety of technologies related to projection, programming, simulation, PERT (program evaluation and review technique), FAME (forecasts and appraisals for management evaluation), assessment, and so on, the project was able to send man to the moon. In addition, factory management technology, such as the just-in-time system of parts ordering and quality control circles, which supports the high productivity of Japanese companies, is worthy of inclusion in the software sector.

Besides the programming and management aspects of intellectual technology, this technology also embraces design and personal philosophy, which are important ingredients in business management, far outstripping the role played by hardware technology, according to the White Paper on Small and Medium-sized Enterprises of 1985.

# 3

# Applications of High Technology

## INDUSTRIAL REVITALIZATION THROUGH HIGH TECHNOLOGY

The recent trend of industrial revitalization in Japan and America, contrasting sharply with the more stagnant situation in Europe, owes much to the positive stance that these two countries have adopted as regards high technology. According to a study by the research department of the Development Bank of Japan, both Japan and the United States have increased their high-tech investments. In the latter half of the 1970s, Japan's capital spending declined in all industries except for this area, while the United States maintained a steady level of investment in all industry sectors.

In another survey conducted by the U.S. Department of Commerce on investment trends in the manufacturing industry since 1983 (1972 prices in real terms), manufacturing investment in the United States recovered sharply from $53.7 billion in l983 to $64 billion in 1984 to $70.7 billion in 1985. Broken down by industry (*see* Fig. 4), investment in high technology as a percentage of total investment stood at a little over 10 percent in the first half of the 1970s but jumped to 19.9 percent in 1982 due to the interest in high technology in the pharmaceutical, computer, and com-

Fig. 4: PLANT AND EQUIPMENT INVESTMENT IN DIFFERENT INDUSTRIES (percentage)

| | | JAPAN | | | | UNITED STATES | | |
|---|---|---|---|---|---|---|---|---|
| | | 1967 | 1975 | 1982 | 1983 | 1967 | 1975 | 1982 |
| Technology-intensive industry | Chemicals | 15.5 | 15.6 | 11.0 | 11.2 | 13.7 | 17.0 | 12.4 |
| | General machinery | 7.0 | 7.4 | 10.3 | 10.6 | 8.7 | 9.0 | 10.2 |
| | Electric machinery | 6.9 | 4.4 | 14.9 | 16.1 | 6.9 | 5.0 | 10.1 |
| | Transport machinery | 12.5 | 9.9 | 16.1 | 14.7 | 7.1 | 7.4 | 12.0 |
| | Precision machinery | 0.9 | 0.8 | 2.1 | 2.0 | 1.6 | 2.1 | 2.8 |
| | Total | 42.9 | 38.0 | 54.4 | 54.6 | 37.9 | 40.6 | 47.5 |
| High-tech industry | Pharmaceuticals | 0.6 | 1.3 | 2.0 | 2.3 | 1.0 | 1.3 | 1.6 |
| | Computers | 0.6 | 1.2 | 2.5 | 3.5 | 0.9 | 1.0 | 3.7 |
| | Radio, TV & communications | 3.8 | 2.0 | 9.3 | 10.3 | 3.8 | 2.8 | 6.3 |
| | Other electric appliances | 3.1 | 2.4 | 5.6 | 5.7 | 3.1 | 2.2 | 2.8 |
| | Aircraft & missiles | 0.1 | 0.1 | 0.2 | 0.2 | 2.4 | 1.3 | 2.5 |
| | Precision machinery | 0.9 | 0.8 | 2.1 | 2.0 | 1.6 | 2.1 | 2.8 |
| | Total | 9.1 | 7.9 | 21.7 | 24.0 | 12.8 | 10.8 | 19.9 |
| | Existing Industry | 57.1 | 62.0 | 45.6 | 45.4 | 62.1 | 59.4 | 52.5 |

Source: Census of Manufacturers, *Annual Survey of Manufacturers*, U.S. Dept. of Commerce; Table of Industrial Statistics, Development Bank of Japan and Kozo Horiuchi.

munications equipment sectors. In the case of Japan, high-tech investment rose throughout the 1970s, reaching 21.7 percent in 1982 and 24 percent in 1983.

By far the most active high-tech sphere is electronics. According to an industry-by-industry survey of changes in the "Top Fifty Companies with Outstanding Performances," conducted by *Nihon Keizai Shimbun*, companies involved in electronics and electrical machinery (*see* Fig. 5), which numbered twelve in 1960, doubled to twenty-five in 1964. And for the next few years, electronics will continue to play the dominant role in high technology.

However, the sector that has achieved the most spectacular progress in recent years is information and communications, which might be regarded as the vanguard of the high-tech industry. Another field that is advancing rapidly is high-tech software, which has a larger market than hardware. However, no software company has made it into the top fifty companies because the industry consists of smaller, venture companies.

Fig. 5: TOP FIFTY COMPANIES WITH OUTSTANDING PERFORMANCES

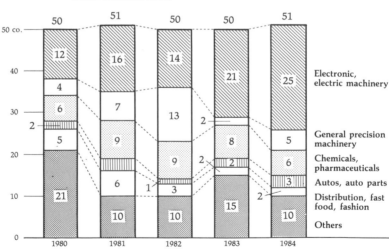

Source: *Nihon Keizai Shimbun*, August 25, 1985.

Nevertheless, they have recorded astounding growth, with the ¥50 stock of companies such as CSK and Intec now being traded for several thousand yen.

## CORPORATE INTEREST IN HIGH TECHNOLOGY

An exhibition of electronics equipment, new materials, and other high technology never fails to draw a large audience, consisting mostly of businessmen, which indicates the high level of interest in high technology. The Economic Planning Agency made a survey in order to find out which technology was most appealing to corporations. The questionnaire asked which high-tech sector businesses were most interested in, and it was circulated among all the companies (excluding those involved in finance) listed in the First and Second Sections of the Tokyo stock exchange. It drew a total of 1,918 responses, or 72 percent. This unusually high response in itself attests to the strong interest in high technology.

The findings revealed that the technology that most attracted businesses (*see* Fig. 6) was information and communications, closely followed by new materials. These two fields each gathered 40 percent of replies, followed by engineering, which covered the entire field of industrial engineering. In fourth place was distribution, the slowest field to streamline operations (in fact, its very backwardness may indicate that it has good growth potential). Other sectors of high technology that appealed to Japanese firms were biotechnology, health care, urban development, leisure-related operations, housing, fine chemicals, new energy, and pharmaceuticals.

Although interest in the next five years is focused on information and communications, toward the year 2000 the picture will change drastically, as the following survey illustrates. The *Nikkei Sangyo Shimbun* questionnaire on the theme of which technology is going to play a central role up to the year 2000 was sent to companies in Europe, the United States, and Japan. The responses showed that biotechnology attracted the most in-

Fig. 6: AREAS OF HIGH TECHNOLOGY OF INTEREST TO COMPANIES

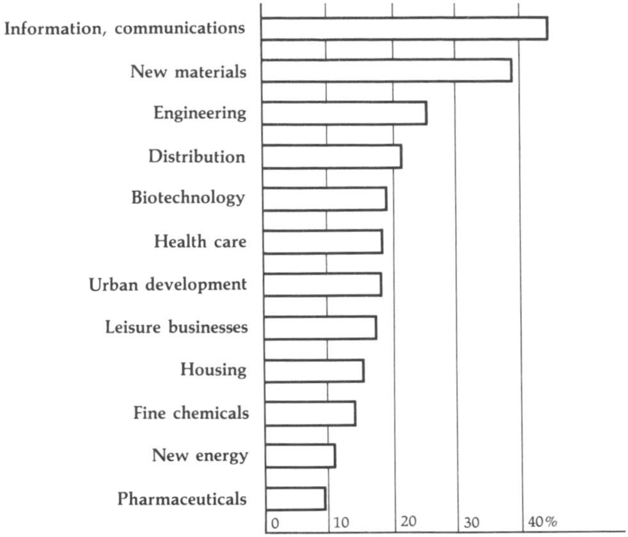

Note: Total exceeds 100 due to multiple answers.
Source: Economic Planning Agency, April 6, 1984.

terest (*see* Fig. 7), especially in Europe, where people seem convinced that an information society will be followed by a biosociety.

The second most appealing sector was computer software, followed by communications, new materials manufacture, electronic parts, and artificial intelligence. This is revealing because here again software technology comes to the fore, and when computers and their related equipment—software, artificial intelligence, and communications—are grouped under a single heading of "information and communications," software again ranks first.

## NEW TRENDS IN ELECTRONIC TECHNOLOGY

Electronic technology—comprising information and communications—is now focused on microelectronics as a result of the sophistication achieved in integrated circuits (ICs). In line with

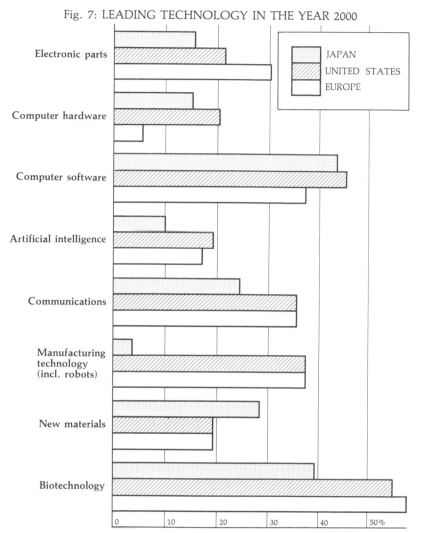

Fig. 7: LEADING TECHNOLOGY IN THE YEAR 2000

- Electronic parts
- Computer hardware
- Computer software
- Artificial intelligence
- Communications
- Manufacturing technology (incl. robots)
- New materials
- Biotechnology

JAPAN
UNITED STATES
EUROPE

0    10    20    30    40    50%

Source: *Nikkei Sangyo Shimbun*, January 1, 1985.

such advancement, the development of electronic technology will spread to a wide range of fields.

After World War II, a variety of new industries and technology came into being, but it was undoubtedly the computer that had the most impact on the business environment. The computer first appeared in 1941, the year the Pacific War broke out, and was produced by the American firm of Univac. This model used vacuum tubes and was about the size of an average room, weighing about one hundred tons. Twenty years later, in 1961, we had the one-chip microcomputer, produced by Intel, with a central processing unit (CPU) one-fourth the size of a fingernail. And from then on progress was even more astounding, culminating in today's 32-bit desk-top computer that can include a variety of peripherals.

The transistor, which replaced the vacuum tube, first made its apprearance in 1948, and measured four square millimeters. In just over two decades, the devices that can be formed on a single chip has been increased by seven orders of magnitude. (It was in 1955 that Sony produced the world's first transistor radio, an event that triggered the company's growth.) Then the transistor was replaced by the IC, and in 1977 the LSI (large-scale integrated) circuit was developed. Today's VLSI (very large-scale integrated) circuit can accommodate one million transistors, and it only measures several millimeters square. The history of the computer is thus characterized by miniaturization and proliferation, and lap-sized personal computers now allow one to work anywhere (*see* Fig. 8).

Conventional technology can only improve the utility factor minimally. For instance, in order to increase the horsepower of a car engine by 1 percent, or the tensile strength of iron by 1 percent, it is necessary to spend ten to twenty years on the project. As regards the computer, however, progress was made in such quantum leaps that its performance improved 1 million times in twenty years.

Electronic technology has achieved a rapid succession of innovations, with each one accompanied by a growth in the electronics market. For instance, since the oil crisis of 1973, Japan's industrial output has been poor, especially in such key industries

Fig. 8: THE DEVELOPMENT OF THE COMPUTER

| GENERATION | DEVICE | USAGE |
|---|---|---|
| 1st 1946–58 | Vacuum tube | Batch operation; programming in machine language |
| 2nd 1959–66 | Transistor | Remote batch operation |
| 3rd 1964–70 | IC | On-line TSS (time-sharing system) |
| 3rd–4th 1970– | LSI | From centralized to distributed processing |
| 4th 1979– | ULSI | Compound distribution processing; database management |
| 5th 1990s | Optimal usable device | Intelligent information processing |

as steel, which in 1973 totaled 128 million tons and today stands at around 100 million tons. Housing starts, too, which stood at 1.3 million in 1973, have declined to 1.1 million today. Compared to these industries, electronics is indeed a horse of another breed. In 1973, the industry recorded production worth ¥4.6 trillion, while in 1983, the recorded figure was ¥12.7 trillion. From both the technological and marketing points of view, the electronics industry has grown astronomically.

However, if you happen to be in this industry at the moment, it does not mean that you can sit back and relax. In size, the IC market is about the same as the market for kimono. However, ICs are not called money-eaters for nothing. They require a huge amount of investment and are subject to wide fluctuations in demand.

Rather, a more important consideration at the present time is not the manufacture of ICs but the application of ICs in your business. The key to future growth lies in how ICs, or microelectronics, are utilized. Depending on how this is done, it is possible to expand a business by, say, one order of magnitude. This is an important rule to remember when planning your business strategy.

To obtain a fairly good idea of trends in the electronics industry, try and visit the annual international electronics fair in Hanover, West Germany. It is the largest such fair in the world and is the size of ten trade fairs put together. To get an idea of its size, if you were to spend one minute at each booth, and six hours per day at the fair, visiting 360 booths a day, you would need twenty days to see all the exhibits. Recent fairs have focused overwhelmingly on electronics, which seem to be developing along the following four lines.

**1. The growth of the personal computer market.**     It was progress in microelectronics that led to the miniaturization and proliferation of the computer, and the functions of these personal computers are reaching the level of the mainframes of the past. In addition, their portability allows you to work wherever you are, without having to go into a special computer room. (This is what I mean by the "distribution," or proliferation of computers.) In the United States, personal computers outsold mainframes and minicomputers in 1983, and this trend is sure to continue.

These compact, high-performance personal computers have completely changed data processing operations. A personal computer is a terminal that is linked to a communications system, which, in turn, is part of a communications network. The development of a communications network, together with the progress achieved in IC technology, has undoubtedly spurred the distribution of computers.

**2. The importance of software.**    No computer can operate without software no matter how sophisticated it is. Even if you are able to purchase the hardware cheaply, it is entirely useless without the software programs. It is no wonder then that Japanese, American, and European businessmen ranked software so high in the previous survey.

**3. The emergence of "new media."**    This term, which may not be familiar to non-Japanese readers, refers to new electronic media for communications, such as INS (information network service) and CAPTAIN (character and pattern telephone access information network), which are popular in Japan and will be dealt with in detail later.

**4. Optoelectronics.**    The combination of optical technology with electronics is increasing, and communications using optical fibers are already in use. In the same way, memory devices such as compact discs and video discs are also gaining popular support, and the same is true of image display technology.

## MICROELECTRONICS

Let us start with the core technology—microelectronics—represented by the ICs that have revolutionized data processing today.

ICs can be divided into two main types: memory ICs and

microprocessors, or gates, for computation. The personal computers available around 1970 were mostly 4-bit models, which means that the computer is able to process four different kinds of data simultaneously. The memory IC used in this model was the 16K RAM (random access memory), meaning that direct access (writing and reading) to stored information is possible at random. With about 1 million devices housed in one chip a few square millimeters in size, the 256K RAM of today has a memory capacity equivalent to a four-hundred-page book.

Japan is the world's leader in the technology of memory ICs as well as their production, with a 92 percent share in 256K RAMs and a 65 percent share in 64K RAMs. This can perhaps be explained by two factors. One, Japan as a nation excels in the technology of integration, where up to one million devices, equivalent to vacuum tubes, are embedded in a VLSI chip. The integration of a number of parts and functions within a specified area is a special skill of Japanese workers. The second reason is that Japan started early on the development of metal oxide semiconductors (MOS), which is an insulating material produced by forming an oxide on the surface of silicon.

If Japan leads in memory ICs, it is the United States that is the undisputed leader in logic ICs such as the microprocessor, or microcomputer, which does computation with logic circuits. As discussed earlier, the single chip microcomputer was developed in the United States in 1961, equipped with a 4-bit processing capacity. This was expanded to 8 bits in 1974, then to 16 bits, and to 32 bits in 1983. It is almost impossible to develop logic circuits without new ideas, and in this area Japan lags behind, having few engineers who are creative enough. However, despite this, progress in IC technology resulted in the cost reduction of IC production, and ICs priced at $360 each at the introduction of Intel's first 8-bit computer are now down to $3 apiece and are still getting cheaper.

In the initial years, ICs were produced by the large manufacturers such as Hitachi and NEC in factories adjacent to their plants in large cities. It was a time when demand was both small and sporadic. In western Japan, Mitsubishi Electric and Matsushita Communication Industrial produced ICs in the Osaka area. These were the first-generation ICs.

With second-generation ICs, demand began to rise, making it no longer feasible to manufacture ICs inside the cities, and new locations with adequate skilled labor and abundant water supplies were sought. It was at this time that IC production began to move to cities on the island of Kyushu. Because of the smallness of ICs, air freight posed no problem, and any city with an airport could qualify as being suitable for IC manufacture. In time, Kyushu became known as Silicon Island, after Silicon Valley in California. By 1984, however, IC production in Kyushu began to decline, due to the building of new IC plants in 1984–85 for the higher-level VLSI circuit, which, in addition to skilled labor and abundant water, required a higher level of technology.

The production of VLSI circuits required facilities that possessed a much more advanced technological level as each chip features up to 1 million devices (and the degree of integration is still continuing). Furthermore, semicustomized products, based on customers' requirements, began to gain ground. This marks the start of third-generation IC production.

With the higher level of technology required for VLSI production came the need for plants to be built close to the technologists who designed them, and thus the Tohoku region, northeast of Tokyo, was chosen as the site after the new Shinkansen "bullet" train service and new expressways to the region were completed. And in time Tohoku became known as Silicon Road after the haiku poet Basho's *A Narrow Road to the Far North*. This move to Tohoku also carried the implication that technology was becoming more important than mere production.

Let me go back to the inapt comparison, in my opinion, of Kyushu with Silicon Valley in California. Silicon Valley is a complex of a number of companies involved in the design of IC circuits and the production of software, as well as having numerous technologists involved in the peripheral aspects of ICs. It is an area characterized by the production of software (intelligence) with a larger market in the peripheral production of hardware (ICs), which is very different from the situation in Kyushu, which emphasized IC production only.

We have talked about how a VLSI circuit a few square millimeters in size is capable of changing our society, but just what can it do? In other words, what are the benefits of such ICs. I shall list them as follows.

**1. High degree of integration.**    ICs contributed to the miniaturization of the computer, and the degree of integration has leap-frogged over the past two decades. This has not only changed the functions of the computer but it has also given new functions to watches, cameras, machine tools, sewing machines, and so on. In other words, it has brought us mechatronics.

ICs come in two types: SRAM (static random access memory)—featuring writing and reading capabilities at any time—and DRAM (dynamic random access memory)—wherein written data expire over a certain period of time. The leader of the semiconductor field today, the 256K RAM, features up to 1 million circuits on a single chip. In a couple of years time, DRAMs are expected to have the storage capacity of 1 megabit, with circuits four times those of the 256K RAM, to be followed by the 4-megabit RAM model, featuring integration four orders of magnitude over the 1-megabit model.

The degree of integration will expand the application of ICs in new fields, in addition to giving us smaller and higher-performance computers and more sophisticated mechatronics. One such example is an electronic translation machine with several English dictionaries stored in a single chip. In the same way, integration has brought changes in teletext, or character broadcasting. At the moment the broadcasting of characters and simple patterns uses "gaps" available on TV broadcasting waves, and when a large-capacity storage is reduced in size, it will become possible to store characters in television sets for reading.

However, there is a line beyond which more integration will produce negative results, and this will happen when the storage capacity of ICs reaches the 1-megabit level (*see* Fig. 9). Increased integration can also prove an inconvenience to users. For instance, a higher integration reduced the thickness of pocket calculators to that of a calling card, with the result that they broke very easily. Moreover, the smaller push pads were difficult for users to hit accurately, making for mistakes in calculating. This is one reason Sharp and Casio failed with their ultrathin calculators.

**2. High reliability.** What would happen, say, if the several million circuits were joined together using the old-type vacuum tubes? Each vacuum tube is inserted into a socket and the lead wires are soldered. You repeat this procedure millions ot times, but trouble will always develop somewhere and it will take a lot of time to locate it. Compared to this, ICs are nearly trouble-free as they are produced by etching on their substrates. IC-incorporated products are highly reliable, and even if trouble does develop, it will not be in the mechanical portion.

Fig. 9: THE RATE OF ADVANCE IN IC INTEGRATION

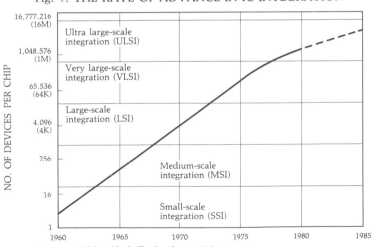

Source: *Nikkei High Technology*, 1984.

**3. Price decline.** At an informal meeting between Mitsubishi Research Institute and the directors of the semiconductor research institutes of NEC, Mitsubishi Electric, Fujitsu, and Toshiba in 1985, it was pointed out that the price of a newly developed semiconductor will be comparable to that of a screw in four or five years. This may sound exaggerated, but semiconductors that cost several thousand yen will decline to around ¥100 in three years. Taking into account increases in the level of integration, which is progressing at lightning speed, the price of a semiconductor will eventually decline to around ¥20 to ¥30.

Figure 10 shows the sharp decline in the price of memory ICs over a short period of time. For semiconductors with storage capacities of 16K to 256K, the speed of decline is even faster. The price of a 64K MOS DRAM went down from $25 in 1981 to $3 or $4 in 1983 and is still declining. Today a computer with the same functions as one in the past costs one-tenth to one-hundredth the latter's price. This steep reduction in price was the main reason for the expansion of the semiconductor market.

Fig. 10: THE PRICE DECLINE OF MEMORY ICs (MOS DRAM)

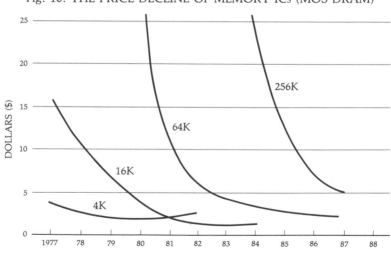

Source: *New Developments in IC Industry,* Y. Shimura.

Which of the following processes in IC manufacture is most profitable: research, production, or application? I often compare the production of ICs to the long-stemmed Japanese pipe, called *kiseru*. The long stem is made of bamboo, while the bowl and mouthpiece are of metal. I like to compare the bowl to the first stage of IC production, i.e., design, which has a high degree of value added and is profitable. The next stage, IC manufacture, is like the bamboo pipe stem; it is hard to make money here as it involves nothing more than manufacturing, which has little value added, and prices are subject to sudden declines. The metal mouthpiece is comparable to the next stage, IC application, such as NC machine tools, robots, computers, and so on. Here there are profits to be made, and Fanuc with its NC (numerical control) machine tools, Epson with its printers, and Sharp with its pocket calculators have all profited from the application of IC technology.

We have seen how the development of the IC has transformed the computer—from the first-generation model using vacuum tubes, replaced by transistors in the second-generation model, to the third-generation computer that used IC technology and the fourth-generation models that use ultra LSIs. In the same way, computer use has also undergone dramatic changes over the years. As the computer became smaller in size, the former centralized data processing gave way to "distributed" data processing, which meant that computers were not confined to a computer room but could be used anywhere, and the resultant proliferation of computers gave rise to a whole new communications network. This step brought with it the complex distributed data processing system. Moreover, with incorporation of ICs in certain machines, there are now industrial robots that do the work of humans and NC machine tools. And this situation is greatly changing the role of functions of a lot of other objects and machinery.

There is no way to avoid a decline in business as long as you stick to the bamboo portion of the Japanese pipe, i.e., the manufacture of ICs. In other words, cities like Tokyo—where research and software production is concentrated—and Yamanashi and Suwa—which produce watches, printers, robots, and other IC-applied products—will continue to grow rapidly in the coming years. Thus, it is not the production of ICs that counts, but the preproduction stage—design and research—and the postproduction stage—application and use, or software.

Carrying the discussion one step further, in which direction is IC technology going after the development of VLSIs? When I was chairman of a special committee of the Science and Technology Agency, a report was prepared in 1984, entitled, "Exploration and Creation of Scientific Technology Relating to Information and Electronics." With the further sophistication in microelectronics the report called for action in the following four fields: microelectronics, optoelectronics, bioelectronics, and software.

With microelectronics, the biggest challenge facing researchers today is the acceleration of computation and processing speed. The semiconductors in use are mostly silicon-based, and, in order to speed up the computation process, it is necessary to change the basic materials or their make-up. Currently, several different types of semiconductors are under study such as "compound semiconductors," which, instead of silicon, use a gallium-arsenide compound that can move electrons faster than silicon.

Another new development drawing acclaim is the "superlattice device," first developed by Dr. Reona Esaki. Ordinarily, metal is in the lattice state, in which the constituent atoms are arranged in an ordered pattern called a crystal. The superlattice device is an artificial alloy, where very thin layers of compounds comprising different atoms are alternatively laminated in sandwich form. For example, layers of gallium-arsenide, indium-phosphide, and other compounds are laminated to produce compound semiconductors.

Research into materials today differs radically from research into materials in the past, when only existing materials were evaluated for possible use. Now, with the predetermined application of materials, researchers "design" a new material that is suited for a predetermined use. Even the way scientists think and tackle technology has changed considerably.

The result of the superlattice device is an IC called HEMT, or high-electron mobility transistor, capable of speeding up computer operations one hundred times. Speed is of ultimate importance today. Suppose a massive amount of computation is needed, for example, in the case of a nuclear power station developing trouble. If the plant is halted for a whole day, there is no alternative but to turn to an oil-burning thermal power station, which costs ¥200 million to ¥300 million more per day in running costs. If the computation time is speeded up, a huge saving in power costs will be realized.

Another category of new semiconductors is the three-dimensional device, which in terms of the number of patent applications, leads all other research projects in this field. The conventional semiconductor is two-dimensional, comparable to a bungalow, so to speak. If the semiconductor can be made into a two- or three-storied house, then it can be densified that much more, and in the future this sort of IC will become important.

What are also gaining importance in semiconductor technology are devices equipped with sensory functions that provide tactile and visual sensations. Another important field is electronic research on molecules using organic compounds.

All the technologies discussed above will see practical application in about a decade or so. The other three areas—optoelectronics, bioelectronics, and software—will be discussed in Chapter Four.

## BIG BUSINESS OR VENTURE BUSINESS?

Venture businesses are springing up in every sector of industry, but unlike the situation in the United States, very few Japanese venture businesses are involved in IC production because of the huge investment required. Japanese venture businesses are small or medium-sized firms that cannot afford this sort of funding; even American venture businesses involved in IC production were gradually taken over by big businesses.

However, there are a number of venture businesses in the personal computer field: Sord in Japan and Apple Computer in the United States come to mind. This is because the computer is a machine that is made up of a large number of parts, and software is all-important. Thus, brain power, not money, carries more weight in the computer world. However, with market expansion, big corporations like NEC and IBM are making inroads into this market, placing Sord and Apple in financial difficulties. With the mass-production of computers, venture businesses cannot fight the giants; instead they will have to concentrate on software.

Where is the computer headed in the years to come? As it has already developed at lightning speed, what sort of developments are possible in the near future?

**1. Reduction in size.**    This entails further development of the so-called small computer, which, though compact, is equipped with outstanding functions. The American firm DEC developed a minicomputer, the VAX 780, that matches the performance of the mainframe of the past. "Compact in size but outstanding in performance," the sales pitch at present, will be even more emphasized in the future.The performance of the new 32-bit personal computers far exceeds what we thought such computers would be capable of.

**2. Increased speed of operation.**    The development of the supercomputer is led by the American firm Cray Research, and a Cray model in my institute several years ago had an operational speed two orders of magnitude faster than current mainframes. Fujitsu and NEC have both successfully developed supercomputers on the lines of Cray, and in the future it is believed that competition will intensify between Japan and the United States in this field. Japan is rumored to win the race as far as hardware is concerned, which will probably spark off another trade dispute between the two countries. However, there is a need for such high-speed computers in business, and the supercomputer will find a promising market.

**3. Superlarge storage capacity.** With databases fast becoming the core of our information society, computers for such use will need very large storage capacities to deal with data. Although databases are slow to catch on in Japan, they are becoming more more important now.

**4. Closer imitation of humans.** Now, thanks to software development, computers have pattern recognition, speech synthesis, and speech recognition functions, as well as are able to emulate the reasoning and procedures of an expert in a specialist field. These intelligent computers will be the computers of the future.

Every scientist dreams of building a computer that is a perfect replica of a human being. At the American pavilion at the Tsukuba Science Expo in 1985, there was one computer that could detect engine trouble in cars, which it managed to do through putting a series of questions to people. The much-vaunted fifth-generation model is provided with such faculties as creativity, inference, and practical wisdom, signifying a departure from the conventional logical process in computers, yet, in fact, it is still far from being a "human being."

Companies buy computers because they are extremely useful machines, but just how capable are they when compared with an employee? In terms of wages, an employee in his twenties costs around ¥5 million a year on average. When his salary rises beyond ¥10 million per year, he becomes part of management, and probably loses his creativity and depends solely on his experience. A mainframe, on the other hand, costs between ¥200 million to ¥300 million in annual rental fees, depending on the model. In costs alone a mainframe computer equals thirty employees, but it can only do standard computation jobs.

In terms of capacity, the human brain measures 1.4 liters, while a computer with faculties similar to those of a human measures about 10 cubic meters. In terms of energy consumed, the human being requires 15 calories of energy per hour, compared to the computer's 30,000 calories an hour. The human brain comprises some 14 billion cells, whereas the computer is equipped with tens of millions of devices. There is no doubt, then, that the human brain is far superior to the computer.

What about storage capacity? Assuming that a single unit of memory equals 1 bit, the conscious brain has 1,000 bits, while the computer has 10 million bits. However, when the human capacity for instant recall, and the memory stored in brain tissues called hippocampus, is taken into account, the human being's memory is 1 billion times that of the computer.

In software, the computer is incomparably inferior to the human being in terms of faculties. The present computer is only able to do what it is told and cannot judge situations or infer from practical experience. This clearly shows the value of an employee over a fifth-generation computer. However, a computer is without equal when it comes to handling routine jobs, and can thereby make business operations more streamlined. But it certainly cannot be used in place of a secretary or an inventor or a boss.

There is one area in which the computer outperforms an employee and that is in the speed of caculation. The human brain requires one-twentieth of a second to make a simple calculation, while the computer can do this in one-millionth of a second, or a microsecond. Moreover, as long as the program is correct, the computer never makes mistakes. It does not need sleep at night, and, above all, it never complains. Provided it is used efficiently, the computer can render invaluable service to anyone's business.

## NEW INFORMATION MEDIA

The information society of the future cannot function without telecommunications, or the exchange of information over a distance.

Today various kinds of office automation (OA) equipment are in use—facsimiles, copying machines, word processors, personal computers, minicomputers, and digital data exchanges (DDXs)—that have freed staff from routine tabulating and filing jobs, allowing them to concentrate more on work that requires creativity, such as research, design, software production, marketing, and production control. There is no doubt that OA equipment plays a central role in the office.

However, such equipment did not function as smoothly as it was hoped in the early stages, and Figure 11 shows the results of a survey on user complaints carried by OA equipment manufacturers in 1984. Ranked at the top were such complaints as poor connection with other equipment, lack of software, and slow communications procedures. Thus the main problem areas in OA equipment lay in software and communications procedure.

When you feed information into your personal computer, it is impossible to pass that information to your branch offices in other regions unless your computer is connected on-line with the computers in those offices. In the coming years, such communications equipment will increase in importance. In the last ten years, shipments of computers have increased fivefold, while computer-to-computer data communications have grown thirty to forty times. As communications systems develop, it will become more feasible to use the computer as a terminal, thereby increasing the number of workstations and popularizing distributed data processing. The number of personal computers used as communications terminals numbered less than ten thousand units ten years ago and is nearing 1 million today, an increase of one hundred times. This trend is expected to continue in the years ahead.

Reviewing the overall growth of computers, communications systems, and small computers that serve as communications terminals, it is evident that the growth rate for small computers is one order of magnitude faster. Due to the advance in communications systems, information processing has spread to many sectors of business.

## Fig. 11: TYPES OF OA EQUIPMENT IN USE

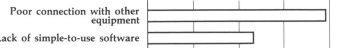

| | |
|---|---|
| Facsimile | |
| Copier | |
| Word processor | |
| Personal computer | |
| General-purpose computer | |
| Office computer | |
| Intelligent terminal | |
| Minicomputer | |
| COM system | |
| DDX (digital data exchange) | |
| Digital PBX | |
| Firm banking equipment | |
| Facsimile communications network | |
| Optical disc file | |
| LAN (local area network) | |
| VAN (value-added network) | |
| Others | |

No. of responses: 746 companies

0    20    40    60    80    100%

Source: *Nikkei Sangyo Shimbun*, December 19, 1984.

## USER COMPLAINTS FILED WITH MANUFACTURERS

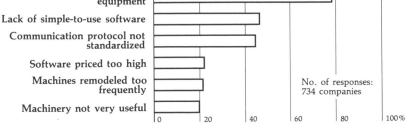

| | |
|---|---|
| Poor connection with other equipment | |
| Lack of simple-to-use software | |
| Communication protocol not standardized | |
| Software priced too high | |
| Machines remodeled too frequently | |
| Machinery not very useful | |

No. of responses: 734 companies

0    20    40    60    80    100%

Source: Same as above.

The problem of compatibility was tackled to eliminate the difficulty of interconnecting different types of OA machines. The computer was first used as an in-house processing system, developing later into an in-house on-line system. This evolved into a new network for the collection and distribution of manufactured goods that resulted in a new system of distribution, as well as a new cash-dispensing system for banks. The problem of incompatibility arose from different business practices, or business protocol, in terms of sales slip formats and merchandise codes. And as long as such systems remain incompatible, progress will be very slow.

Two solutions are possible to overcome this. The first calls for the standardization of business protocol, carried out at the same time as equipment standardization, and the second solution calls for the establishment of an industry-by-industry network that allows for systems compatibility through the "conversion" of business protocol. Without such a network, it will be difficult to achieve a sophisticated information society.

This communications network is certain to bring forth changes in industrial organization rather than changes in industrial structure. In other words, it is the content of industry that will change. In finance and distribution, for instance, simultaneous access to the same information in different regions, as well as direct links between manufacturer and consumer, will be realized. This will affect transactions between manufacturers and subcontractors, and smaller businesses will have exposure to a larger market. This is not to say that all sectors of industry will benefit from a communications network, however.

The systems that are generating intense excitement in Japan are the new information media, capturing the attention of both the mass media and businessmen. The Japanese have caught media fever, it seems, as firms jump to join the CATV and CAPTAIN systems in anticipation of the profits the new market will bring.

However, how lucrative is the new information field and does it deserve the kind of response it is generating? Frankly speaking, I find it overrated, although there are some profit-making possibilities in store. It is more correct to say that the new media represent a jumble of wheat and chaff, and I will take up the major systems for discussion.

**1. The Information Network Service (INS).** This service provided by Nippon Telegraph and Telephone (NTT) is a member of the new media family, although it is not really new. The vice president of NTT, Yasusada Kitahara, who was responsible for its concept, explains that INS is an integrated information network system, comprising telegraph, telephone, data communications, and facsimile networks. The advantages of INS are: the elimination of the problem of distance; the reduction in communications cost and the rationalization of the rate system; and the establishment of convenient and varied services. When signals and charges are unified, it will become possible to offer other services to users.

INS is expected to register steady growth for two simple reasons. First, there are 40 million telephone users in Japan, and these telephones, which will become communications terminals, are usable after the full installation of INS. Thus NTT already has a built-in market. Second, INS represents a technological advance in that digital transmission is faster and more efficient because, in the case of the telephone, it operates on codes, not sound waves, as in analog transmission. Such digital transmission will also be applicable to facsimile machines and data communications.

Digital signal transmission will also eliminate the need for separate lines for telephones, facsimiles, and data communications, making all communications possible via a single line. This integrated network of communications marks the real strength of INS. There is an international plan to install a global integrated network called ISDN (integrated services digital network), but this system differs from the Japanese one in that it has a number of computers incorporated in the network to provide a "conversion" mechanism. France is the leader in the digital communications field.

For INS, there are plans to switch to fiber optics communications or satellite communications in order to increase capacity. Optical fibers, which are the thickness of a hair, have the transmission capacity of six thousand telephone lines. In 1985, a trunk optic fiber cable was laid in Japan to link Asahikawa in Hokkaido (in the north) with Kagoshima in Kyushu (in the south). An undersea cable is also being laid between Japan and the United States, making it possible for low-cost, large-volume communications in the future.

The INS has a number of advantages because: the market is well established; digital communications allows for the transmission of a number of signals via a single line; information can be handled in volume by optical fibers and satellite communications; and costs are reduced and regional communications gaps eliminated.

How is price going to be affected? For instance, telephone charges for the CAPTAIN system, which I will discuss later, are fixed at ¥30 for three minutes irrespective of distance, making it possible to send a lot of information at a low cost. This will, in turn, expand user access to the service. In addition, image communications, hitherto prohibitively expensive, will become a possibility.

**2. Videotex.**    Also known as CAPTAIN in Japan, NAPLPS in the United States, Telidon in Canada, Teletel in France, Bildsilm in West Germany, and Prestel in the United Kingdom, it is a character and pattern information request service that works through telephone lines. In Japan hundreds of businesses rushed to become information providers under the CAPTAIN system because they smelled profit. However, this system has run into some snags.

When we talk about the CAPTAIN system entering the average household, most people think that it will allow them to do their shopping and banking from the home. In reality, it is debatable how useful or satisfactory the information provided really is, and except for France, videotex has been slow to gain consumer acceptance.

Take home banking, for instance. In general no Japanese household needs to go to the bank every day; twice or three times a month is sufficient. Moreover, in a small country like Japan that is well equipped with shops, direct shopping is easier to do than shopping by the CAPTAIN system.

The American Videotron system developed by AT&T went into commercial use in Florida in 1983, and in a three-year period it managed to win 2,600 households. This situation is similar to CAPTAIN, which is used by 700 householders, most of whom belong to the monitor group in Mitaka. In the United Kingdom, videotex is also faring poorly, and information for the general public is apparently not commercially viable.

However, it is too hasty to write off videotex entirely as it does have certain uses in some sectors, where it can be a profitable concern, for example, the presentation of specialized financial information such as that provided by Dow Jones. Dow Jones operates the database, which is connected to personal computers (there are 16 million in the United States) and telephone lines to provide up-to-the-minute quotations on stock prices, dollar rates, gold prices, and so on. Supposing 1 percent of the population in the United States is interested in such information, that means a market of over 2 million people. Dow Jones information service subscribers are growing at a rate of two thousand every ten days.

When compared to the Videotron service, Dow Jones's success in the information service is evidently attributable to such differences as the quality of information, subscribers' needs, and the quality of equipment used.

The second sector where videotex is successful in is business-use information, such as information needed by travel agents and real estate agents. A travel agent will find the CAPTAIN system very useful when making ticket reservations for clients; likewise, the real estate dealer can easily produce floor plans of houses on a CRT display. This sort of information service is immensely popular in the United Kingdom, and businesses are now turning to videotex for in-house information.

The third sector where videotex has strong growth potential is in government-sponsored information services. This sort of service is already provided by the French government in the form of Teletel, the electronic telephone directory. The French government has also developed a videotex known as Minitel for free leasing to the 1 million telephone subscribers in 1985, and this figure is expected to treble in three years. In France, where 20 percent of the population changes telephone numbers every year, this service is more economical than producing new telephone directories every year. In addition, the widespread use of videotex resulted in an increase in telephone revenue (the government's investment in Minitel is said to have been recovered in two and a half years) as well as an increase in the amount and type of information provided.

In conclusion, it can be said that the videotex market varies according to the type of information provided, and depending on what sort of information is in demand, profits will also differ. Despite the drawbacks of the CAPTAIN system in Japan mentioned earlier, videotex will become viable in this country if it is used by businesses to provide specialized quality information, particularly information where time is an important factor.

**3. CATV.** Originally this referred to a common antenna TV system, developed to overcome problems of receiving television signals with one aerial in a designated area. However, somewhere along the line CATV came to mean a cable TV system, and the most popular is the two-way CATV.

In two-way CATV, audiences can partake in TV programs through the TV station. However, commercially this system just does not work. At one time there was a CATV station in Columbus, Ohio, known as QUBE, the first such station. When I visited the United States in 1985, I found that it had already gone out of business. When I talked with a former participant, I got the impression that the novelty wore off after six months.

If used in Japan, two-way CATV is sure to suffer the same fate because Japanese television viewers already have a choice of programs from eight channels. One cannot expect them to get involved in TV shows as well. Moreover, a CATV station would need to hire more staff for such an operation, so this is definitely not a good commercial proposition.

On the other hand, a one-way CATV system looks more promising. Also known as multichannel CATV, the American system works by transmitting TV pictures fed by a key station via a communications satellite to local ground stations, from where the images are transmitted to subscribers via cable. The system incorporates a number of exclusive channels dealing with weather forecasts, sports, religion, news, and so on. Since two-way communications are not involved, there are less expenses as no extra personnel are needed.

In the United States, 97 percent to 98 percent of CATV stations have abandoned two-way operations in favor of multichannel operations. Furthermore, most of these companies are making a profit from TV commercials now that CATV is more popular. The government-backed ordinance for the protection of CATV businesses has also helped. In 1984, subscriptions covered 42 percent of households that own TVs, an indication that CATV can be resuscitated by switching from two-way to one-way operations, by the rationalization of in-house business operations, and by the protection of the government ordinance.

One area where CATV is strong is in providing clear images and sound by eliminating interference from neighboring TV stations. The Netherlands, in particular, suffers from constant interference from German and French broadcasting stations, and the common antenna TV is proving extremely popular, with as many as 60 percent of households using it.

What are the prospects for CATV operation in Japan? At the moment it is being used by private railway companies and supermarkets, who are interested in the two-way communication system. I told one executive of a private railway company about the dismal prospects of such a system. He agreed with me but added, "If we say our tracts of housing land for sale are equipped with CATV, then the cultural status of that land will rise and we can make a far bigger profit than the losses incurred in setting up CATV." Well, that's one way of looking at it, perhaps.

**4. Satellite communications.**   These are used far more in the United States than in Japan, which, because of its size, is not so interested in this mode of communications. It is highly feasible, however, for distances over five thousand kilometers, and this is most suited for international communications. Satellite communications allows for the simultaneous transmission of news reports around the world, and the nationwide transmission of "USA Today" in the United States is producing good results.

However, a look at the largest satellite operator in the United States, Satellite Business Systems, shows years of operation losses, reflecting the difficulties of domestic satellite communications. On the other hand, two new developments in this field look promising: mobile satellite communications (to and from moving units like ships and trucks), and teleports, or external communications bases, using satellites. There are, for instance, seventeen parabolic receiving antennae set up on Staten Island for optical fiber communications with Manhattan. In the future, teleports may well replace airports as the ports of entry into a country.

**5. Packaged media.**   These differ from the INS, CAPTAIN, and CATV systems—which all rely on the use cables as their mode of communications—in the sense that packaged media feature only the "media." The most popular examples of these are video cassettes and video discs, which are also known as laser discs.

Video cassettes are sure to register substantial growth in the years ahead. Five or more years ago, the best-selling cassettes in the United States were pornography, but today this is down to about 10 percent of total video sales, while movies, music, and other types of entertainment are gaining in popularity. Jane Fonda's shape-up exercise video has sold hundreds of thousands of copies. These sales might not seem substantial when a book can sell over 1 million copies, but the profitability comes from the fact that a video costs ten times the price of an average book.

Video cassettes have a huge rental market. In the United States they cost a dollar a day, so it is both cheaper to rent a cassette and less dangerous than going out to the movies at night. The new 8mm video cassettes will undoubtedly play a part to spur growth in this market over the next few years.

The video disc, or picture-producing disc, come in two systems: one is the electrostatic capacity system and the other is the laser system. RCA was once involved in the development of the former type, but it abandoned it halfway, leading many Americans to believe that it is an inferior system.

The other system utilizes a laser beam for the writing and reading on the disc, which is shaped like a gramophone record, with fifty thousand grooves, each with an image. Thus a disc is capable of recording the same number of images, which is equivalent to two hundred books. It is ideal for recording encyclopedias and other reference books.

Video disc players are still too expensive, but once their cost falls below ¥100,000, these machines will proliferate phenomenally. Recently a new player has been introduced that can take both video discs and compact discs (for sound only).

Regarding the future of packaged media, Video Shack, the largest such wholesaler in the United States, commented that, compared to CATV, packaged media will continue to grow, and many industry people are predicting that the laser disc and the 8mm video disc will replace CATV in time.

# 4

# New Directions for the Future

Continuing with our survey of technological innovations that are expected to play a leading role in the future (begun in the previous chapter), we will examine the current progress in optoelectronics, or the technology of light, in new materials technology, in new machine technology, as well as consider which technology will become most essential in the twenty-first century. Will it be biotechnology, as some industry people believe? The present-day applications of such technology, as well as its future direction will also be examined.

## OPTOTECHNOLOGY

We are living in a very visual age in Japan, evidenced by the fact that one weekly comic (*Shonen Jump*) has a circulation of 4 million copies. Other weekly photo news magazines are selling briskly, and images are a far more attractive vehicle of communication with today's youth. The technology that is indispensible to the age of images is optotechnology.

This light-related technology is evident in a multitude of fields. The result of a survey listing optotechnological products in order of market share revealed that products in the optical fiber communications field recorded the largest share, the major ones being light transmission equipment, video discs, laser printers, laser processing machines, light-emissive diodes (LED), and quartz fibers. Fifty-five percent of those polled predicted that the opto-industry market will be worth a staggering ¥2 trillion in 1990.

The development that has had the greatest impact in the field of optotechnology is, without doubt, the laser beam. Light consists of rays of varying wavelengths, apparent in the seven constituent colors of light, and the laser beam is produced by making light monochromatic, or of a single color, with uniform mountains and valleys. Thus the laser beam develops waves that are similar to a radiowave, and it is capable of performing the same function as the latter. Furthermore, its short wavelength is equal to one-hundredth an ordinary wavelength, and laser waves can be used to transmit information. The greater the number of waves in light, the more information it can transmit, and laser waves are capable of transmitting over one hundred times the information that ordinary radiowaves can handle. This explains why laser beams are used in such a variety of fields apart from communications and information.

The combined technologies of optical fibers and lasers have given us optical communications. We might picture optical fibers as the "blood vessels" that carry information and laser beams as the "blood" that carries this information. If you examine the structure of an optical fiber, you will find that its chief component is quartz. The core of the fiber is covered by a clad that is also made of quartz. The core and the clad have different refractive indexes. Light passes through the core, and since the fiber consists of two structures with differing refractive indexes, it is reflected within the fiber and does not escape. In short, the fiber features little damping characteristics.

Conventional light transmission requires a relay every kilometer, with an amplifier, which sends it further. The underwater electric cable between Japan and Hawaii used several thousand relays; but the number of relays required for the optical undersea cable that is now being laid by KDD has been reduced by one order of magnitude. This, and the capacity of optical fibers for transmitting information in volume, means that optical technology is perfect for communications use. However, fiber costs are still high, and conversion and connection technology is still lagging behind, although in time these bottlenecks should be cleared.

Another light-related technology is the display of images such as fluorescent display tubes, electroluminescence (EL), liquid crystal display, cathode ray tubes (CRTs), and plasma display panels (PDPs). In order to determine which one of these will predominate in the future, one has to consider the size of the display area and the resolution of the images. Liquid crystal displays, CRTs, and PDPs are good for large-area displays, while electroluminescence and fluorescent display tubes are better suited for small-area displays. The sharper the image the greater the increase in pixel pitches. High-resolution CRTs and high-definition TVs have greater image sharpness compared to plasma and liquid crystal displays.

In the field of memory discs, a variety is now available, such as bipolar RAMs, MOS RAMs, magnetic bubbles, magnetic drums, magnetic discs, and optical discs. The way to evaluate such memory discs is by access time, or how fast the required information can be retrieved, and the cost. Discs that use ICs, such as RAMs and magnetic bubbles, feature faster access time but higher costs, while magnetic drums, magnetic discs, and magnetic tapes cost less but require more time. Superior to these by far in terms of access time and cost are optical discs, indicating their potential in the future for memory use, such as filing.

Other applications of optotechnology can be seen in laser printers, used as computer peripherals, which have the twin merits of high speed and good reproduction quality, and laser measuring devices that, because of the short wavelength used, have a high degree of accuracy. Another advantage is that they do not need to be near the objects to be measured. At the 1985 Hanover trade fair, Daimler-Benz had a laser that could measure the combustion state of engines. Incorporated with a liquid-level meter, lasers can accurately measure the deflection of bridges and other structures, as well as the wind-caused deflection of steel frames, such as those used in the Honshu-Shikoku bridge that connects two of the main islands of Japan.

Optotechnology is also applicable to various other fields such as laser processing, which is a promising market. Laser beams are powerful enough to cut through thick sheets of steel, and their destructive force is evident in the U.S. Strategic Defense Initiative, commonly known as Star Wars, where ground missiles can be destroyed accurately within a three-hundred-kilometer range.

Another development is the application of lasers to the field of energy, typified by nuclear fusion energy, which uses the heat generated by the fusion of superhigh temperature plasmas, based on the principle of the sun. Another new system, in which laser is used to gather plasma particles, is now attracting attention from all quarters. Laser is also used for the separation of radioactive uranium to produce enriched uranium, and the United States is planning to replace the conventional method of enriching uranium with this system. With the development of amorphous solar cell technology, solar cells will also gain new uses, thereby greatly reducing the prices of such devices.

With such a variety of technological potential, optotechnology will undoubtedly succeed electronics as the next core technology.

## NEW MECHANICAL TECHNOLOGY

Compared with the many new developments in electronics, communications, and new materials, no spectacular breakthroughs have been recorded in machine technology. One region where progress has been achieved is in composite products, or hybridization, where high technology is incorporated into such machinery as tools, electric appliances, cameras, testing equipment, automobiles, copying machines, and medical instruments. This development has affected the machinery market considerably.

Aside from hybridization, another trend has emerged that will affect the future development of machinery, and this is systemization. This refers to the integration of a number of functional elements—such as electronics and electronic parts, machinery and machine parts, or communications—into a machine. Videotex, for instance, will not work without the database, telephone line, CRT display with modem, and software. All of these are systemized products. Systemization can be seen in such sectors as plant engineering, banking, the Shinkansen "bullet" train service, and the information network service (INS). NASA's rocket to the moon is a systematized project comprising some 5 million individual products.

Another application is urban development, represented by the Tsukuba Science City, produced by the construction of laboratories, houses, and other living-related facilities at a cost of ¥800 billion.

If one course open for the development of mechanical technology is the hybridization of machine-electronics composites, followed by the systemization of various machines, then another course is found in robotics. Robots have up till now been employed mainly by auto makers and machine tool manufacturers in such jobs as welding and painting. Today's robots are equipped with advanced, intelligent functions, such as visual and speech recognition. Robots of the future, like those seen at the Tsukuba Science Exposition in 1985, will walk, play musical instruments, and paint portraits. In short, their functions will closely echo human functions.

There are robots today that can do various jobs, such as Fanucman, a giant robot that does assembly work, or a robot that can spin a top on the edge of a Japanese sword, or a robot that reacts to what we say. Despite these advances, the robot, aside from its efficiency, still has certain limitations. And these limitations serve to remind us what a fine piece of precision machinery the human being is. Robots cannot react realistically to the situation at hand, for instance. Fanucman, which assembles robotic parts, will say "Well done," even when it drops a part. Robots cannot respond to speech with a regional accent, neither can they play an instrument with emotion. Fanucman weighs twenty-five tons and can lift a two-hundred kilogram barbell. Before you register astonishment at this, didn't the 1984 Olympic gold medallist perform the same feat? And he only weighed around one hundred kilograms. Human beings are incredibly powerful pieces of machinery too.

Another trend in machine technology, apart from robotics, is computerized support. In a *Nikkei Mechanical* survey conducted in April 1984, people were asked what high technology they would like to see in practical use in the next five years. The answer that ranked at the top was computer-aided design (CAD). Among the many uses of CAD, the most popular are automatic design drawing, human intelligence techniques, and the projection of the life span of machine parts. In second place was flexible manufacturing systems (FMS), or fully automated production lines for manufacturing varieties of the same goods in small quantities. This was followed by a LAN (local area network) linked to CAD, which automatically detects if anything is wrong, and a computerized system of production. In third place came robots, particularly for dangerous work, equipped with simple language understanding, and low-cost multipurpose robots. Ranked fourth were machine tools, in particular tools that automatically adjust fabrication conditions when they are put into operation, laser-processing machine tools, and NC (numerical control) machine tools.

Thanks to CAD, CAM, and FMS, engineers today need not stay up all night drawing plans on a drafting board, and so their productiveness is improved. CAD is not, however, limited to the drawing of plans. Aided by a computer, it can simulate the conditions for a wind tunnel test, say, or measure the strength of an aircraft at its design stage. Also it can produce clay models of automobiles and measure them, feeding the data in a computer so that cross-sectional views of the car are possible for display on a CRT screen from any angle. CAD is also becoming a powerful tool in designing IC circuits and molds. Despite claims from American businesses that CAD is too complicated to operate, many smaller businesses in Japan are using it.

The top executive of a foreign computer company in Japan remarked that computers for CAD use are more common in Japan than in the United States. Similarly, robots are more widely used by smaller Japanese companies than in America. However, in software it is the United States that is still the leader, even in CAD.

Japan is more advanced in FMS, also known as simple automation—comprising computers, robots, machine tools, unmanned carts and warehouses—that allows the user a flexible production line capable of turning out different products on the same line. Gerald K. O'Neil, author of *Techno-Nationalism: The Electric War* (Shinchosha, 1984), was surprised by the efficiency of such a production system, particularly in the Yamazaki Ironworks plant, which turns out over seventy different kinds of lathes and machine tool parts. Such FMS plants are common in this country.

With the market shift away from mass-produced goods to diversified goods, flexible reprogrammable automation with the computer playing a central role is growing rapidly. However, let us not neglect the role of design too in machinery, especially in durable goods like the automobile and household appliances. Although two cars may be identical in performance, one will sell better if it is better designed.

At the Hanover trade fair, my impression was that mechanical technology showed two tendencies: scaled-down size and good design. Machines are getting smaller, lighter, and more portable, and the same can be said of automobiles. The compact Mercedes-Benz is selling well in Japan, as are compact TV cameras and portable personal computers. As far as design is concerned, the Hanover trade fair exhibits that are awarded Good Design prizes all share the qualities of simplicity and refinement. The Europeans are definitely the leaders in design, with a preference for curved lines that costs more in molds, whereas the Japanese favor straight lines that have lower mold costs.

NEW MATERIALS

Materials can be roughly classified according to their features into structural and functional. Materials like steel and cement that are used for structures are classified as structural, while materials like magnetic materials and semiconductors that are provided with specific functions are classified as functional.

When we speak of materials, we automatically think of steel and aluminum, which are both faring poorly today. However, this common mistake stems from our concept of conventional structural materials. The manufacture of materials has not declined, but the situation is completely different when you look at materials manufacturers who have switched to functional materials. Take iron, for example. Growth has halted for iron and steel manufacturers involved in the production of iron as a structural material. However, producers of iron products called ferrites, and magnetic materials made from ferrite, are all experiencing rapid growth. The same situation is found in the cement and brick industry, which was once very brisk and is now on the wane, while manufacturers of functional materials such as new ceramics for IC packaging and capacitors are enjoying continuing growth despite the similarity in the manufacturing processes, namely, sintering rocks and minerals from the earth.

Structural materials in which strength is the sole value are expanding their range of application, as in the case of engineering resins developed from new materials, but it is also a fact that demand for such products will eventually decline. On the other hand, although demand for some functional materials—generally referring to magnetic, electrical, chemical, and biological materials featuring specific physical and chemical functions—is on the wane (such as for plastic and vinyl chloride materials), demand for others, such as functional polymers, is growing. One of the uses of functional polymeric membranes is now being studied at MITI's

Research and Development Project of Basic Technologies for Future Industries. An oxygen-enriching membrane, which takes only oxygen from the air, it features air permeability for the separation of oxygen, constituting a target for the development of functional membranes. Biocompatible and conducting polymeric materials also belong to functional materials, which, by and large, is a most promising field for the future.

There are two main reasons for this bright prospect. One is a change in industry. Structural materials are for the construction of machines, and since machines are getting smaller, lighter, and more compact, less material is required to make them, thereby lessening demand for such materials. Compounding this state of affairs is the halt in the growth of engineering and construction industries. At the same time, as information and communications become more prominent, there is a demand for new features such as intelligence and more sophisticated machines. Functional materials have ample room for growth because they support such improvements, as reflected in the varying growth rates of the two types of materials. The second reason why functional materials have more future is that technological advances in them can occur much faster, and this speed of progress is giving rise to new products, thereby also expanding demand.

Shown in Figure 12 is a chart indicating the technological advance made in permanent magnetic materials, with the magnet's coercive force as a barometer. Chromium steel was in wide use until KS steel was developed. The former had a coercive force of 50 kilo Oe, whereas the latter's was 200 kilo Oe, and Alnico 5, also known as Mishima steel, has a coercive force of 500 kilo Oe. Ferrite, first developed by Takeshi Takei and Yogoro Kato, was quickly followed by the development of a variety of new ferrites, which have registered amazing progress. Type 1. 5 SmCo features a coercive force of 7,000 kilo Oe, and a rare metal magnet comprising niobium, iron, and boron has a coercive force of 11,000 kilo Oe, about two hundred times that of a magnet of fifty years ago.

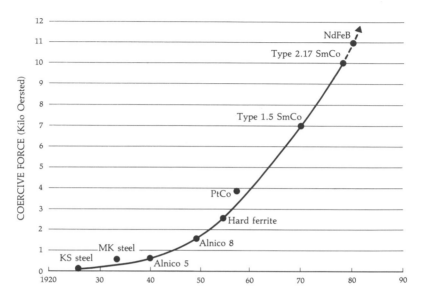

Fig. 12: THE DEVELOPMENT OF PERMANENT MAGNETS

By comparison, progress in structural materials is snaillike. To-day nickel-chromium-molybdenum steel is used for its strength despite the fact that it has only been improved 20 percent to 30 percent in the last few decades. Piano wire has improved 20 per-cent in fifty years, while copper alloys, aluminum, and alloys have increased their tensile strength only marginally. Thirty years ago I lectured on metallic materials at Tokyo University, and the textbooks I used then show that the capability of structural materials in those days is not much different from their capability today.

However, it should be clear that what is being discussed here is nothing more than growth potential, or profitability, of the two types of materials. In terms of market size, structural materials are by far the leader despite the fact that they are begin-ning to decline.

What is the growth potential of functional materials and what sorts of materials are they? I shall list them as follows.

**1. Semiconductor materials.**    Gallium arsenide compounds used for compound semiconductors are one of the new functional materials under study for next-generation semiconductors.

**2. Magnetic materials.**    These are valued for their applications in diverse fields ranging from computer memories, speech and image recording, and speaker magnets. In recent years a gadolinium alloy used in optomagnetic discs is attracting attention. The alloy is used in erasable optical discs because of its characteristics: when heat is applied to a magnetic disc with a laser, the disc loses magnetism in the heated portion but regains it when cooled.

**3. Rare earth metallic materials.**    These are represented by lanthanum-nickel and iron-titanium hydrogen-storing alloys. The alloys are fantastic metals that contain hydrogen, and they are now used as fuel tanks for automobiles on an experimental basis. Hydrogen is used as a fuel, but a hydrogen cylinder carries the risk of exploding. That's why metals capable of absorbing and releasing hydrogen are at the technological forefront today.

Niobium-tin and vanadium-gallium alloys are characterized by their loss of electric resistance when cooled to very low temperatures. One of the applications of such alloys is in the linear motor car developed by the former Japanese National Railways. The linear-motor car uses a superconductive material, which, having no electric resistance, develops a powerful magnetic force when current is applied to the material. This car is the train of the future, made to float and travel at high speeds through magnetic force. It is believed that a superconductive phenomenon, if achieved at temperatures above those of liquid hydrogen, will change the design of electrical machines completely. There is also talk of a shape-memory alloy. For instance, a nickel-titanium alloy, bent into whatever shape, will recover its original shape at a certain temperature. However, no appropriate uses have been found for this alloy yet.

**4. Fine ceramics.** New uses for ceramics in electronic parts have given rise to many fast-growing companies today. With the super heat-resistance of fine ceramics, new types of machine materials are being put into practical use. The most important of these are silicon nitride, silicon carbon, and zircon oxide materials, which, unlike brittle conventional ceramics and earthenware, are both tough and heat-resistant. They are expected to find uses in diesel engines and turbines and in knives and safety razors. Kazuo Inamori, chairman of Kyocera, said that its safety razors proved so long-lasting that Kyocera finally stopped making them because the consumers did not buy replacements.

New functional materials employ a variety of new metals whose names and origins are even puzzling to me, a scientist and technologist. However, it may be useful to list the new targets of research in this direction to get an idea of what is going to happen in the future. In 1984 the Science and Technology Agency founded a committee to locate targets for basic research in this field and I was involved in setting up such targets. The committee report, "Creation and Exploration of New Substances and Materials," cited six items, the first three of which are for laboratory research and the other three are the uses such materials can be put to.

The first research target was to find new bonding methods for atom-comprising substances, in addition to such present methods as covalent bonding, ionic bonding, and metallic bonding. The second target was to explore new reaction mechanisms, such as mechanisms where the application of light could step up certain chemical reactions. In addition, ultrafine particles and catalysts are used to promote reactions between substances, thereby producing a new material. The third target was to theoretically design new materials and produce them. Using a computer, the properties and compositions of materials and substances were studied for the design of new materials. Superlattice devices and HEMT (high electron mobility transistor), for example, were produced through analysis of several materials and compounds of indium, phosphorus, gallium, and arsenide, thereby producing new combinations.

The next three research items deal with actual experiments with such materials and their usefulness to businesses. The first one involved the effect of extreme climatic conditions, designed to create metals in different climatic environments. For instance, the synthesis of metals under the conditions of weightlessness might produce materials with different characteristics, such as homogeneity and nondefectiveness, compared to those produced in the gravity state. The synthesis of metals in a weightless state, called a microgravity state, has already been experimented on in an artificial satellite. Also experiments on the use of superhigh temperature plasmas and the synthesis of diamond and boron nitride (cutting materials) under superhigh pressure have been conducted. A phenomenon where electric resistance disappeared completely at cryogenic temperature, and a superfluid phenomenon, where a fluid permeated glass, were confirmed in a series of experiments.

The second practical research item was to find out the utmost limit to the control of shapes and purity, thereby potentially producing new materials. The research has shown new physical properties, such as the state where crystal atoms are arranged in a defect-free state (perfect crystal) or in a completely disorganized state (amorphousness). Extremely thin membranes and filaments, microfine particles, and extremely pure metals and semiconductors also have interesting properties.

The so-called amorphous metal is the biggest research theme among metal-related researchers today. Ordinarily, a metal features atoms arranged in a definite form. When the metal is melted at a high temperature and cooled at an extremely high velocity of 1/10 millionth-second, for example, the atoms in liquid and disorganized form are solidified without forming a crystal as they are unable to recover their original shape. This state is known as the amorphous state, and a wide variety of amorphous materials are being developed for use in magnetic, solar cell, anticorrosive, and other applications.

The third practical research aim is the production of composite materials, or new materials by compounding the characteristics of two existing materials. High-performance materials are being developed by compounding ceramics and organic materials, in addition to metals. Hybridization, where different microfine substances are dispersed in materials on the atomic and molecular level, is also a new research subject.

With all that is happening in new materials, it is tempting to give up the steel business, say, and join the new functional materials industry. However, this would be very premature because the market is still not large enough. In a study of the market size of new functional materials, MITI made the following projection for the year 2000.

The total market size for new functional materials is estimated at ¥5.3 trillion—¥1.5 trillion for polymeric materials such as polyamide, photosetting and thermosetting resins, and foaming resins, ¥0.4 trillion for composites such as carbon fibers and boron fibers, ¥1.5 trillion for metallic materials such as amorphous metals and single-crystal alloys, and ¥1.8 trillion for nonmetallic materials such as fine ceramics and optical fibers.

This may be a shock to some, but it is correct. In the year 2000, Japan's GNP is projected to reach ¥600 trillion, with industrial production doubling GNP because duplicate accounts are involved. The new materials market represents only about 1 percent of GNP despite the fuss made over it now. The market for conventional materials is projected to reach over ¥50 trillion in the year 2000; however, it would be impossible for conventional materials to reach the targeted amount if improvements are not made. A steel plate, for instance, which is now a minimum 1.1mm thick should be thinned to 0.7mm; synthetic fibers should be finer, enabling the production of synthetic furs. Improved in these ways, the conventional materials market could be ten to fifty times greater than the market for functional materials.

Nevertheless, new potentials and high added value are the characteristics of functional materials, and their per-unit price and profit ratio far exceed those of existing materials. Great hopes are set for new functional materials despite the limited market potential of such new products and their profitability.

New technologies, which are played up by the media with increasing frequency, will have to be satisfied with their small market share as long as they remain unused. The market for VAN (value-added network) in three years from now is estimated at ¥100 billion, or roughly one-third the miso-paste market. Likewise, the IC market is projected to remain the same as the market for the casting and foundry industry. In industrial areas the new technologies play a small role, but it is expected to grow as the existing industries change. The leading-edge technology fever is a malady particular to Japan, but it also represents one of the country's strong points.

## TECHNOLOGY FOR THE TWENTY-FIRST CENTURY
### Biotechnology

Two or three years ago in Japan everyone was singing the praises of biotechnology or space technology, with the media spinning tales of new products manufactured by gene recombination techniques or new space factories producing new types of goods, and so on. These are still very much in the realm of science fiction, however. The eagerness with which the Japanese jumped on the space bandwagon is said to astound the Germans, who, being a practical race, believe in leaving all future plans in the hands of the government and concentrating on producing machinery and parts that emerge from the development of these plans. This is the proper order of approach, I feel.

However, in the broadest sense of the word, biotechnology will be without doubt a core technology of the twenty-first century, with various uses such as bioreactors, which further the conventional bacteria-based fermentation process of saké and miso by a continuous industrial production with new bacteria and immobilized enzymes. Another way biotechnology may be used is for the production of artifical organs. In Japan, however, most uses of biotechnology are seen in genetic engineering, of which the major ones are the following.

**1. Gene recombination.**    Gene recombination is one of several genetic engineering techniques, where, for instance, human genes are incorporated into the genes of the bacteria E. coli and B. subtilis to produce growth hormones, insulin, and interferon. E. coli have outstanding reproductive capability, with 1 bacterium multiplying to 20 million overnight.

This is extremely valuable for the production of insulin, used in treating diabetes. The insulin in use today is extracted from pigs, and there are cases of incompatibility in some patients. However, genetically engineered E. coli will produce human insulin in large quantities: a culture tank the size of a desk will produce enough insulin for the whole world.

**2. Cell fusion.**    One way of manipulating artificial genes is through the technique of cell fusion, which is responsible for the "pomato." When the cells of a potato and a tomato are stripped and fused together, the genes of the two vegetables are intermixed, and the new plant will produce tomatoes above-ground and potatoes below-ground. However, at present, they are said to be lacking in taste and they do not produce seeds.

Cell fusion technology can be more realistically used to improve plant strain and to allow plants to grow in adverse weather and soil conditions, such as tomatoes in cold climates and potatoes in the tropics.

Another instance of the use of cell fusion is seen in hybrid rice, a crossbreed strain that is tougher and yields more than ordinary rice. Just as children of mixed blood parents are more attractive and inherit the best sides of both parents, hybrid rice is an improved strain that yields as much as one ton per ten acres of farmland. However, because these properties are not passed on to the next generation, new seeds are always needed. In a country that has a surplus of rice such as Japan, hybrid rice can be more of a problem than a blessing, but seed companies are nevertheless making the most of this cell fusion technique.

Today there is a process whereby parts of a plant can be made to propagate by means of tissue culture. For instance, gromwell, which is highly valued as a medicinal herb and a dye, is tissue-cultured to produce *shikonin*, a pigment used successfully in the manufacture of biolipsticks.

*Bionics*

Biotechnology is subject to various definitions depending on the country, and for this reason I would like to define it here as technology relating to the improvement or utilization of organisms. Bionics also suffers from various different interpretations, one of which even covers a variety of related technology such as biomimetics and biomechanics. Bionics can be defined as technology that imitates mechanisms of living things to produce new products or new technology. It is more readily applicable and has a larger market than biotechnology, which is limited to gene manipulation.

Living organisms behave in mysterious ways, and bionics attempts to imitate some of these strange modes of behavior. Take the life cycle of slime molds, or myxomycetes, for instance, a kind of amoeba. Usually slime molds live independently, but when there is a shortage of food due to changes in weather, they gather in a cluster, which in time hardens into a mass. The mass gradually starts growing into a tree shape, and the molds on the upper portion of the tree are dispersed by wind or other animals to places where food is available, while those at the root stay behind and die. It always seems to me that the molds themselves are involved in such role decisions.

There is also talk about holistic management, whose theory is not to regard the whole as a sum of its parts. Just like the cells of an organism, the parts have some relationship with one another, building up to develop a function as a whole. The life cycle of slime molds presents a study in a holistic way of living.

Bionics is designed to make the best use of the mysterious workings of living organisms. Salmon are a good example. They never fail to return to the river where they were spawned, although no analysis of that water has given us any clues as to why this should be. Salmon that are sprinkled with the water from the river they were spawned will start moving energetically. Apparently, they sense something we cannot trace, just as butterflies can exchange information by scent even when separated by a distance of two kilometers.

Not all animal behavior may be clear to us, but through research, we are able to make better use of that information in bionics. Rattlesnakes cannot see but they feel infrared heat, which makes them spring at humans and animals. Bats emit ultrasonic waves to avoid obstacles in their path of flight. Based on this research, scientists have produced spectacles that enable a blind user to avoid obstacles in his path through ultrasonic waves. In this way a blind marathon runner was able to place third in a race, and a blind motorcyclist was able to ride about in traffic.

The mysteriousness of living organisms can extend technological potential into a wide variety of fields, and some examples of the application of bionics are listed in Figure 13. One such biomechanism is a biomotor. The human body is a very efficient machine. On a bowl of rice, we move and jump by means of muscles, which consist of two myofibrils: actin and myosin. When a chemical substance called ATP is decomposed on the tip of myosin, myosin and actin start a tug of war, thus bending the arm as desired. The biomotor acts on the same principle.

Actin whiskers are planted onto a vane comprising mica, teflon, and polysin, and this is placed in an aqueous solution containing myosin. Actin on the vane reacts with myosin in the solution, and thus they repulse each other to rotate the vane. Such analyses of living organisms and life will become more important in the future.

Fig. 13: A SUMMARY OF PRESENT-DAY RESEARCH IN BIONICS

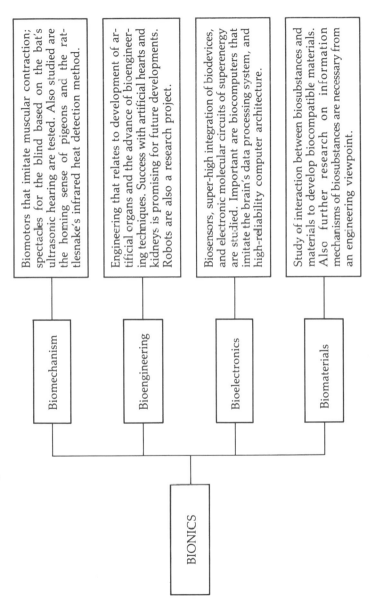

Source: Noboru Makino, Mitsubishi Research Institute.

## Space Technology

In countries like the United States, Europe, and Japan, it is the government that takes the lead in space development. Technological developments undertaken by private business are few, except for communications satellites and a few other examples. Over the coming years, however, space technology will offer greater possibilities of developing into major businesses, so we need to outline some of these developments.

Presented in Figure 14 is a time schedule for space development projected by Professor Tatsuzo Ohbayashi at the Institute of Space and Astronautical Science. Space development has progressed from the launching of the Sputniks in the 1950s to the space shuttles of the 1980s. For the 1990s, there is a projected construction of a space station to house scientists indefinitely. This is to be followed by the construction of a large-capacity solar power plant and mass-production plant, with a space colony or space island in the next century.

Fig. 14: A TIME SCHEDULE FOR SPACE DEVELOPMENT

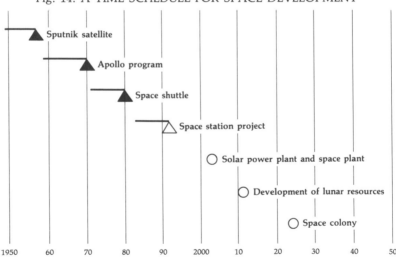

Source: Tatsuzo Ohbayashi, Institute of Space and Astronautical Science.

The solar power generation project calls for the launching of huge solar cells into space to gather solar rays, sending back this energy to Earth via microwaves. A solar cell measures two kilometers by four kilometers, and one cell is capable of supplying enough electricity for the entire city of New York. Despite its size, its construction and assembly, done in weightless space, will not take long. However, this is still too removed from practical application to be more than a dream project at the moment.

The projected space factory is for production carried out in a weightless and supervacuous state, which may become an effective method for the manufacture of special substances, perhaps heralding some major technological breakthroughs. However, such production operations are extremely costly, so they have not progressed beyond the research stage.

The space colony is envisioned as a huge space station to house hundreds of thousands of people built at the Lagrangian points in space, where gravitational forces of all the celestial bodies are in a state of equilibrium. However, like the space factory, it is far from realistic because of the huge investment involved.

What businesses use most are the communications satellites, such as Intelsat and Inmalsat, without which efficient, fast, and low-cost communications are impossible. What will follow from these satellites are weather satellites, expected to become reality in a few years, and earth remote-sensing satellites. However, there is one important factor to be remembered, and that is that 70 percent of artificial satellites in use are designed for military purposes. Thus, a vast gap exists between the peaceful utilization of space and the military use of artificial satellites.

The Strategic Defense Initiative in the news today will be able to shoot down missiles, within minutes of their being launched, with laser or electron beams discharged or reflected from a space satellite. However, the project is another decade from realization and will require over ¥20 billion in research funds. This is one example of how the market for space development today is dominated by the military.

*New Energy Sources*

Whenever we talk about energy, it is always accompanied by a discussion of oil prices or the supply of oil. In the year 2000, crude oil is expected to fetch $62 a barrel, over three times its current price. Meanwhile, wholesale prices by then are projected to grow by only 4 percent. With adjustments made for inflation and other factors, the price of crude is estimated at around $29 a barrel in current terms by the year 2000. If we make a forecast with the present rate of crude standing at $20 per barrel, the real price of crude is expected to remain unchanged, or decline, if nothing critical takes place.

What is worthy of attention in the field of energy is the advances made in the diversification of types of energy. Supply bases have increased, and the Middle East is no longer the world's sole oil supplier. At one time 70 percent of the world's oil supply passed through the Straits of Malacca, but this is becoming history today. Energy has become diversified, with focus shifting from petroleum to natural gas to nuclear power.

With oil prices remaining unchanged, and with sources of energy supply becoming more diversified, and with the development of alternate types of energy in progress, we can deduce that there will be no future oil crises. However, if we want to know what direction future energy technology is going to take, we should look at the results of a survey (*see* Fig. 15) that polled over one hundred specialists conducted by the Energy and Resources Subcommittee of the Science and Technology Agency's "Delphi Projection of the Year 2000." It lists five top items among over seventy subjects relating to energy and resources.

In order of importance, the items are: 1. storage and control technology for solidified high-level radioactive wastes; 2. the fast-breeder reactor (FBR) system, including the recycling of nuclear fuel; 3. technology for the safe disposal of solidified low-level radioactive wastes into the atmosphere and the ocean; 4. technology for the closure and dismantling of nuclear-power

Fig. 15: ENERGY TECHNOLOGY SURVEY OF SPECIALISTS

| Order | Item | No. of Replies | Importance (%) | Time of Realization |
|---|---|---|---|---|
| | | | | 1985 1990 1995 2000 2005 2010 |
| 1 | Application of storage and control technology for solid high-level radioactive wastes | 124 | 92 | |
| 2 | Development of fast breeder reactor (FBR) system, including nuclear fuel production | 109 | 91 | |
| 3 | Application of safe disposal technology for solid low-level radioactive wastes in the atmosphere and ocean | 128 | 91 | |
| 4 | Application of technology of closure and dismantling of nuclear power generation facilities | 108 | 89 | |
| 5 | Realization of large-scale commercial nuclear fuel recycling plant | 107 | 88 | |

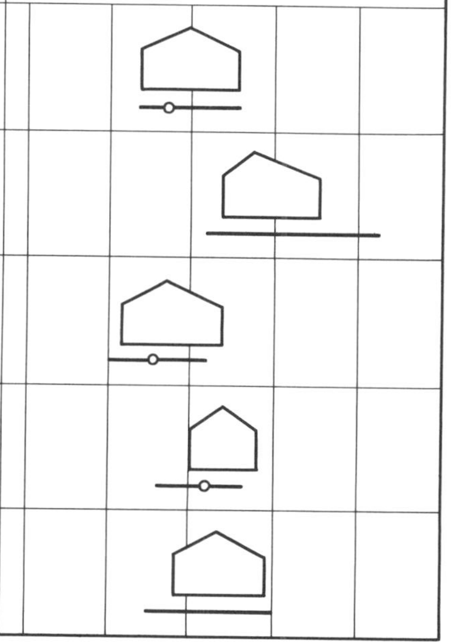

Source: Energy & Resources Subcommittee, Science and Technology Agency, December 1982.

generating facilities; 5. large-scale commercial nuclear-fuel recycling plant.

These results, more than anything else, show that the biggest tasks relating to resource and energy technology are the issues of nuclear waste disposal and nuclear-fuel recycling in nuclear-energy processing.

In conclusion, I would like to repeat that there is no doubt that high-tech industries—which despite their small size are continuing to grow with vigor—will support the economic activities of a country. These industries may not be the main factor behind economic growth, but they do act as a catalyst for growth by invigorating the economy. For example, the tiny IC has played a key role in the progress made in automobile electronics, which, in turn, led to growth in the automobile industry.

A recent viewpoint holds that high technology actually plays a supporting role in certain core industries, which has a lot of truth in it, as the following quote from *Iacocca*, by Lee Iacocca (Bantam, 1984), illustrates:

> Frankly speaking, I have no doubt that high technology will be important for the future of American industry. However, the United States will not be saved by high technology alone. The growth of high technology, to a large extent, can only occur as a result of the purchase of high technology by industries that are not in the high-tech field. I do not want you to misunderstand my statement. High technology will be extremely important in the future for the American economy. However, even though it is important, high-technology industries definitely will not be able to absorb as many working people as are presently employed by the main industries. Recent developments in the textile industry have taught us this lesson.

High-tech industries in the declining sectors of the textile industry were only able to absorb 2 percent to 3 percent of the laid-off workers. Moreover, as Yutaka Takeda, former president of Nippon Steel, says: "Although we may well be on the threshold of an advanced information society, we cannot live on information alone. The information age is sustained by industries such as electronics and computers, which are, in turn, supported by the steel, aluminum, electric power, and energy industries. It is correct to describe the brain as the most important part of the human body; yet neither the head nor the body can live if the two are separated."

Regarding such high-tech industries as the IC and new materials industries, the products they make are only a part of the materials used in the whole product. The price of the IC in a watch or camera accounts for only 3 percent to 5 percent of the product. Such industries involved in the production of electronics parts are also called "percentage industries" since they are used in only a certain percentage of the whole assembling industry.

It is not a mistake for an enterprise to turn completely to high technology. Even the healthiest of industries are taking pains to look for new business opportunities by adaptations in operational procedures to incorporate this small technology. However, the point I wish to make is that too much is expected of high technology. One could attribute these high hopes to Japanese vitality; yet the result of this might spell disaster for Japan's industries. Evidence of this danger abounds in the recent cases of failures among high-tech ventures.

We have already described the way companies have rushed into frontier industries such as ICs, new media, or biotechnology. The present situation is akin to ten people jammed in a tub designed for three. Manufacturers hurried into robot production, new media, and shape memory alloys, only to give them up one after the other.

This has occurred not only in frontier industries but also in other industries, and it constitutes a pattern of behavior dating to the past. Companies will bear the discomfort of being squeezed in a crowded tub with the hope that eventually the other seven will be edged out. However, at times like these it is important to take the courageous step of getting out. The reluctance of doing this is obviously understandable in a manager who has strongly urged his company to enter new fields. Yet knowing when to withdraw is just as important as knowing when to advance. The more I observe cases of frontier industries being run aground by stagnant demand, the more keenly I am aware of how crucial it is to take a bold step back and change course. A businessman has to know how to protect his assets and cut his losses.

# 5

# Developments
# in Software Technology

WHAT IS SOFTWARE?

If I want to drive from Ginza to Shinjuku in half the usual time along the crowded streets, what are my choices? I could build a new road, and for this I would need steel pipes, concrete, engineering equipment, and so on. This represents the solution offered by hardware, based on technology that assumes a shape or a form, such as machinery. Alternatively, I could realign the traffic signals or gain the necessary information to allow me to select the least crowded streets. These are the solutions offered by software, or "formless" technology, which is speedily advancing in importance in society as well as in business.

Technology today is divided into two categories, namely, software and hardware, and it is software that is more valued at the moment. In 1955, the cost of computer hardware, or data processing equipment, accounted for over 80 percent of the total cost. In 1985, however, sales recorded by software manufacturers exceeded those registered by hardware manufacturers. In addition, software sales have become an integral part of hardware manufacture, for rather than just producing computers, manufacturers are also preparing programs and developing systems to make optimum use of their equipment. This is how drastically the picture has changed in just thirty years.

The reason for this change can be seen in Figure 16, which shows the relationship between the number of functions per IC circuit and the cost of each of these functions. In IC manufacture, design costs play a large part since the greater the number of functions, the more time is needed for its design, resulting in higher costs for such ICs.

However, with increased integration, per-unit costs for IC assembly and testing have come down. Whereas a decade or so ago, the hardware costs involved in circuit manufacturing were far greater than for software, their positions have been reversed. In general, focus has shifted away from hardware to software, and in the search for the optimum use of the high-tech industry, software is becoming even more important still.

What constitutes software? In order to find out, a survey was conducted by the Small and Medium-sized Enterprises Agency focusing on elements of manufacturing regarded as important by

Fig. 16: THE RELATIONSHIP BETWEEN COST AND
NUMBER OF FUNCTIONS OF ICs

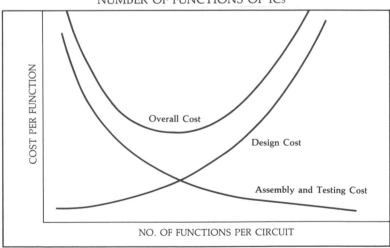

Source: *Nikkei High Technology*, 1984.

such businesses (*see* Fig. 17). Did they place more emphasis on hardware or on software in their operations? Hardware elements include manufacturing facilities, human resources employed in them, raw materials, and energy. Software elements include human resources in technical and administrative departments, design, software, and marketing know-how.

The results showed that those businesses that gave priority to hardware totaled over 95 percent before the first oil crisis of 1973. Each oil crisis was accompanied by a decline in this figure, which, after the second oil crisis, dipped below 80 percent.

In contrast, businesses that placed priority on software elements have increased rapidly. Before the 1973 oil crisis, the figure stood below 70 percent, soaring to 85 percent after the second crisis and eventually surpassing the percentage giving priority to hardware. Thus, we are, beyond doubt, in the age of software.

Today the manufacturing industry employs less workers in its plants and more employees working on design, marketing, software, and production control. This job change is another reflection of the switch from hardware to software.

Fig. 17: TECHNOLOGY RATED IMPORTANT BY SMALL AND MEDIUM-SIZED MANUFACTURERS

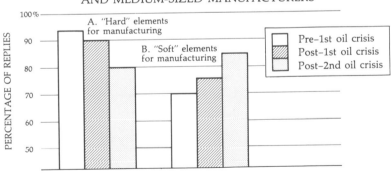

Note: "Hard" elements are manufacturing facilities, line personnel, raw materials, and energy. "Soft" elements are technical staff, design, and marketing know-how.

Source: Management Strategy Fact-Finding Survey, Small and Medium-sized Enterprises Agency, December 1983.

## APPLICATIONS OF SOFTWARE

Some fifteen years ago, when a recessionist mood was prevailing in the watch business as the market for wind-up watches had reached saturation point in Japan, Hattori Seiko was having a very difficult time. In shipbuilding, automobile, and steel industries, when the domestic market reached maturity, new markets were sought abroad, and this is what Seiko attempted. However, the world market at that time was dominated by Swiss watches, so this was not easy to do.

In time, however, something happened that changed Seiko's future. The first electronic watch incorporating an IC was developed by a Seiko subsidiary, Seiko Epson. Although Seiko is not an IC manufacturer, it developed a new product that utilized ICs, and in this way Seiko was able to create a new demand. At around the same time, the first Casio digital watches made an appearance, which also represented a remarkable business advancement.

In short, what I wish to say is that it is better to become a maker of products incorporating ICs than an IC manufacturer. There are all kinds of Japanese products on the market today incorporating electronics now that machine technology has come to a standstill. We call this "mechatronization." Many companies that had excellent machine assembly technologies used this as a springboard toward the incorporation of high-quality ICs in their machinery. Such mechatronized products from Japan have rapidly penetrated markets the world over.

Cameras are one example. German cameras may be outstanding pieces of precision machinery, but they do not incorporate electronic parts to the greatest extent possible. Taking advantage of this "gap," Japanese cameras have flooded the world market. Other examples of such mechatronization are NC (numerical control) machine tools, which are being used by manufacturers all over the world.

I often add the suffix "tronics" to aspects of our present society. Apparel, for instance, can be apparel-*tronics*, banks can be money-*tronics*, gas companies can be gas-*tronics*. In other words, through the application of electronics to various business sectors, something new will eventually come into being, and the bridge spanning electronics and the "something new" of the future is software.

In terms of market size, machinery incorporating ICs, or mechatronics, is much larger than for just ICs, as mechatronics has revived the entire machinery market. And at the risk of repeating myself, I urge you to look for ways of utilizing high technology rather than develop it, for the clue to success lies hidden in the application of high technology.

The same applies to "new media." NHK, the public radio and TV station, once showed a program on how farmers in Canada have reaped the benefits of new media by relying on videotex (Telidon in Canada) for weather and market information. They knew when to expect frost and in which areas, which markets would pay the best prices for vegetables, and so on, all of which allowed for quick changes in planting and transportation plans.

In Japan's Nagano Prefecture, farmers cooperatives are using similar techniques to prevent gluts in the vegetable market. They collect nationwide information on the market situation via new media and transport their produce to areas that will pay the best prices. They are also able to hold back surplus vegetables, releasing them again when needed. Sowing times are monitored, and even crop yields can be improved with the aid of advanced technology.

*High Technology and the Service Sector*

In the corporate world, the effects of such technology would undoubtedly be greater than in agriculture, and it would be adopted by industries over and above the manufacturing industry. The industrial structure of Japan is often compared to Shinjuku Station's west exit, where several huge skyscrapers exist alongside one- or two-story dwellings. The manufacturing sector boasts of high technological capability and high productivity, but in other fields such capability and productivity are nonexistent.

One sector in which productivity lags far behind is Japan's tertiary industry. Compared with international levels of productivity, the manufacturing sector alone rates highly (*see* Fig. 18). In the commercial, financial, and service sectors, there is ample room for improvement. And the way to achieve this is by transferring the advanced technology developed in the manufacturing industry to the service sector.

The 1984 White Paper on Trade describes the impact of information technology on tertiary industry, detailing how efficiency can be improved through the adoption of certain information technology. The following list shows some technology that has been adopted.

> 1. Distribution—on-line system distribution between buyer and affiliated retailer; introduction of POS (point of sale) terminals.
> 2. Finance—on-line operations between head office and branch offices; on-line cash dispensers under a tie-up agreement.
> 3. Transportation—systemization of transportation control, office administration, and distribution departments; and the formation of networks.
> 4. Tourism—formation of a network of related companies centering around such transportation industries as railways and air lines.
> 5. Advertising—utilization of new media such as CATV and videotex.
> 6. Newspapers—rationalization of production processes by such means as the introduction of cold-type printing, photocomposition, and the launching of database operations.

In the above suggested areas for improvements in efficiency, the common denominator is the hookup of networks between related industries. The distribution and tourist industries are

Fig. 18: A COMPARISON OF INTERNATIONAL
PRODUCTIVITY LEVELS

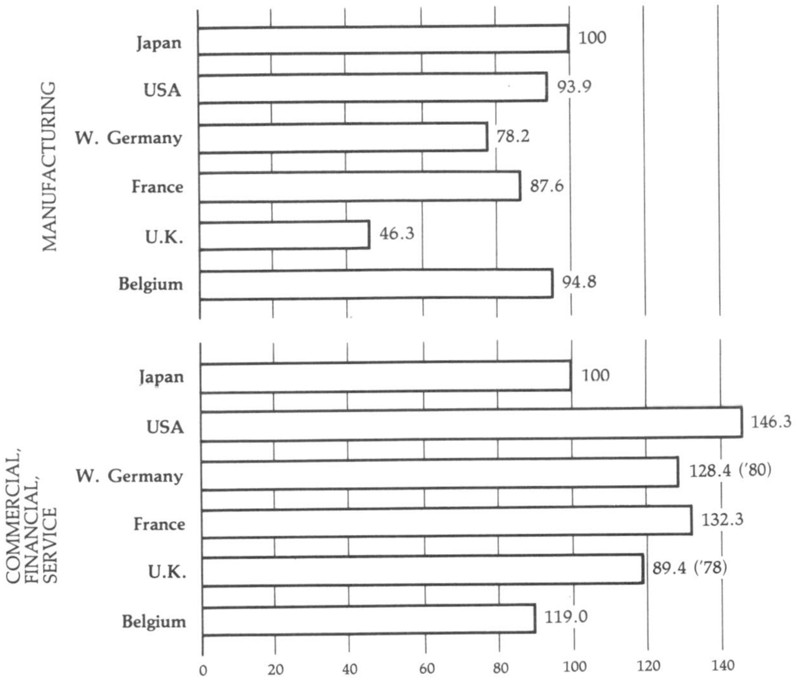

Note: Per capita/per annum GNP (standard); 1981=100
Source: Japan Productivity Center.

waiting for an increase in the number of household terminals to
enable them to exchange information directly with families. The
newspaper industry is aiming at publications for remote areas
through the use of communications satellites, and electronic
or facsimile newspapers have already been tried at the 1985
Tsukuba Science Expo by *Asahi Shimbun* and *Nihon Keizai
Shimbun*.

## VAN (Value-added Network)

Among all the new media, the one that corporations expressed greatest interest in is VAN, or the value-added network. Originally, VAN was the name of a business that operated by borrowing communications lines, turning analog signals into digital signals, and then placing them in a "bucket." This collected information was then transmitted. The advantage of VAN lay in the low fees that users paid for the amount of information received. However, it is gradually getting into communications hookups among different types of businesses and into data processing operations. Thus, the meaning of VAN has expanded, and in Japan all such communications are now called VAN.

In the United States, sales recorded by companies such as Time Net or GTE Telenet, which offer "mixed" communications services, i.e., services that have data processing features, such as various types of computer access services (known as VAN here), account for less than 1 percent of total sales recorded by the entire telecommunications service. It totaled ¥120 billion in 1986.

In Japan the sales of NTT are about ¥4 trillion, of which 90 percent is accounted for by telephone charges, with most of the remaining income coming from in-house on-line operations. VAN as a communications business is represented by NTT's DDX-P and Intec's ACE Telenet, but the market is still small even though the industries that use VAN, such as the distribution industry and pharmaceuticals, are huge ones.

Intec's president, Koji Kanaoka, who pioneered the VAN business in Japan has said that sales of his company's ACE Telenet, the only VAN service available for private sector use, registered annual sales of ¥1 billion, and this figure is expected to treble in three years. This amazing growth is due to the combination of data processing with communications services, making it possible for such diversified services as transportation and distribution to work efficiently. Along with decontrol and market expansion, an increasing number of businesses in adjoining areas are taking part in the VAN business. In the United States a network service of AT&T's called NET100 and one of IBM's called IN (information network) were offered a few years ago. As the fields of data processing and communications services are as yet limitless, it is high-level functions that determine the competitiveness of the data processing supplier.

## NEW TRENDS IN SOFTWARE DEVELOPMENT

At Tsukuba Science Expo, the Fujitsu pavilion generated a lot of excitement with its three-dimensional movie. The huge screen extended onto the ceiling and measured over twenty meters across, and on it the birth of living creatures was projected by means of computergraphics. One billion yen was spent on preparing the graphics software, while the Omnimax projector only cost ¥360 million. The invisible software was three times more costly than the hardware.

A survey conducted by *Nikkei Sangyo Shimbun* inquired which would be the leading industries in the future by polling Japan's leading scholars, critics, and businessmen. Twenty-one of the respondents listed electronics first; followed by nine replies citing the information industry. Only two replies listed the auto industry, and none named any heavy industry. Those who cited other industries, including the service industry, numbered six. Thus, everyone is aware that electronics is at the core of future industries, such as communications, OA (office automation) equipment, and computers. From this we can assume that information software will become of the utmost importance in a short span of time since hardware is not functional without it.

Regarding the size of the software market in the United States, in 1990 it is expected to total some ¥5 trillion, equivalent to 2.5 times the size of the hardware market. In other words, in three years the software market is expected to exceed that of hardware by a wide margin, growing at average annual rates of 20 percent until 1990. On the technical side, Japan is five years behind the United States, and the software industry is expected to grow from the present ¥2 trillion to ¥3 trillion in 1990.

The term "software industry" covers a whole range of diversified functions. It is the technology that makes best use of the information equipment centering around the computer. It can calculate the strength of materials or make system analyses for client companies. These services can be termed "information processing." There are firms that make "packaged software" for shared use among certain computers, and there are firms that dispatch programmers to businesses in need of such services, as well as specialty service companies that provide consulting services on optimal network systems. Software is also a part of the manufacture of computers, but most software businesses are still small venture businesses.

In line with the expansion of the software industry, there is a growing movement by computer manufacturers to vertically integrate software industries. In the United States, there are many cases of computer manufacturers "marrying" software firms or placing software firms among their affiliates, and this is happening in Japan.

Bearing in mind that the development of software engineering is directed at improvements in productivity through industrial manufacturing operations, we should define this demand and clarify its specifications. Also, it is necessary to put programs in modules and make them standard products of the manufacturing industry, completing this by combining the products under a "total system." As for design, the future leads us toward the structure of a knowledge-based system that allows for automatic design.

With the rapid increase in the volume of software products, it will become important to develop technology for their maintenance or for recycling them. This is an important research target and should be included in the initial stage of production. Lastly, as in the manufacturing industries, the instigation of quantitative quality control of software is needed, as well as the preparation of some future guidelines.

*The Software Industry in Japan and the United States*
When we compare the situation of the software market in Japan

with that in the United States, we find some startling differences. For instance, packaged software does not sell well in Japan for reasons unknown, and there are only a handful of businesses using such software. However, in the United States, more than half of all software consumers rely on packaged software. Users there adjust their businesses to the software, and if their efficiency suffers slightly as a result, that is disregarded. In Japan, users prepare their own software, and there are a lot of firms looking for such custom-made software.

On the technical side, the United States is ahead of Japan, and you may remember the shocking case of Japanese companies spying to get hold of IBM's secrets. Computer companies in Japan, except for NEC and a few others, were manufacturing computers that used software that was compatible with IBM software, and impatience on the part of Japanese manufacturers led to their trying to secure the software quickly in this way. The fact that Japanese manufacturers produced computers that were compatible with IBM products is itself a sign that Japan could not compete with the United States, and in the future the Japanese software industry's success will depend entirely on whether it can strengthen its competitiveness.

## IMPROVEMENTS IN STANDARDS

The type of software that is attracting most attention both in the United States and in Japan is that developed for artificial intelligence, or AI, use. With AI software, a computer is able to recognize the human voice and understand some speech patterns (see Fig. 19). By 1990, Japan's AI market is estimated at ¥10 trillion and, although this seems overoptimistic to me, it nevertheless promises to be vast.

One particular AI application that will have a large market share in the future is the "expert system." As the name suggests, this is a system provided with expert knowledge in a certain field, such as medicine or engineering. The most popular exhibit at the American pavilion in the Tsukuba Science Expo featured an ex-

Fig. 19: THE APPLICATION OF ARTIFICIAL INTELLIGENCE

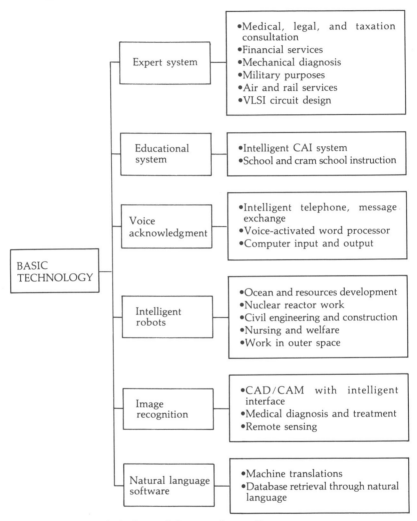

Source: Mitsubishi Research Institute System Department.

pert system capable of diagnosing malfunctions in automobiles and transformers. Equipped with very sophisticated software, the computer, like a patient seeing a doctor, responded to a series of questions, from the answers to which it made a diagnosis.

Some time ago Mitsubishi Research planned to establish an "Artificial Intelligence Project," and it invited other companies to participate in the research. Surprisingly, sixty companies took part, each paying ¥600,000 in fees. This shows the sort of interest generated by this particular field.

In the United States, artificial intelligence is a booming field, and even Dow Jones wanted to incorporate AI into its information network services in order to improve the level of replies, evidence that the use of AI is not limited to manufacturing.

The other promising fields are computer-aided design and manufacturing, and compatible database systems. Such a database system can only be used as a communications network with a modem, which allows communication between different models of computers. For both computer-aided design and manufacturing, and compatible database systems, the biggest problem lies in how to align the databases. The type of information stored and the ease of retrieval are the main considerations. Previously, a database would contain the information in books and periodicals; however, the new generation of databases has made it possible to record information in the computer's magnetic tape, store it, and call for it when needed from an on-line terminal, eliminating the need to go to libraries and the like.

The United States has the most advanced database setups, with a number of large databases on-line, and I often make use of it in Japan. I receive the data through international communications services, paying a fee ranging from a few hundred yen to over one thousand yen for each piece of information I receive.

In this area Japan still lags considerably behind. Mitsubishi Research is the sole agent for NTIS (National Technical Information Service), which offers various database services. However, sales are still low.

Computer-aided design, or CAD, is making much progress recently because the design data is stored in the computer's memory, making it possible to design while watching the stored data. It eliminates the need for work at a drawing board, thus shortening design time. It also enables one to prepare charts or tables by using a plotter or printer. Three-dimensional CAD, for complex drawings, have made design work relatively simple.

Computer-aided manufacturing, or CAM, prepares specifications for the manufacturing process. Using CAD data, CAM prepares NC (numerical control) tapes for automated machine operations. The pioneers in this field are General Motors and Lockheed, and in the 1970s CAM was much utilized in the manufacture of ships, cars, and ICs. The software used in the initial CAD and CAM systems was either American-made or was developed by the manufacturers themselves. And again, in software, the key to CAM, the United States is far ahead of Japan.

Computergraphics is expected to be more widely used, and software development in this direction is sure to gain in importance. Computergraphics, or the visual form of CAD, have extensive applications, and with the Cray supercomputer, Mitsubishi Research was able to do graphic work for SF movies and for TV commercials titles. It can also be used to show the movement of fluids in a nuclear reactor or a chemical plant by means of "visual simulation," and it is now being used for safety analyses of industrial plants.

## THE SOFTWARE CRISIS

With the progress of software comes an accompanying search for technical experts, and it is standard practice to pay a recruitment fee of ¥2 million to ¥3 million in hiring one such specialist, evidence of the scarcity of experts. A survey entitled "A Forecast of the Gap in Software Supply and Demand in Japan," published by MITI (*see* Fig. 20), showed that Japan in 1986 had about half a million software specialists, no real shortage. However, the situation in the year 1990 will be quite different. In the next few years, calculating that demand for software technicians will increase at an annual rate of 26 percent, by 1990 there will be a need for 1.6 million software specialists. Compared to this, the

Fig. 20: THE GAP BETWEEN SOFTWARE DEMAND AND SUPPLY
IN JAPAN

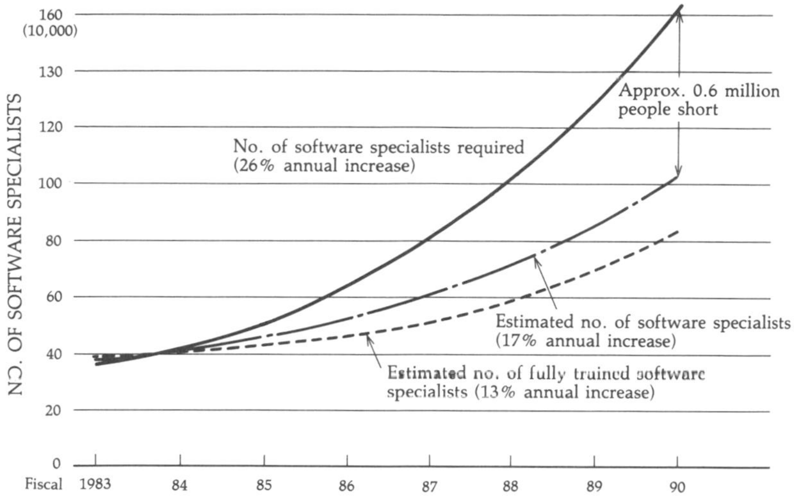

Source: Ministry of International Trade and Industry.

actual annual increase in the number of such experts is only 13 percent. Consequently, there will be a shortage of over half a million software specialists by 1990, which will, in turn, affect the computer market.

One reason for this crisis is the growth in the total number of computers. Computer programs are being produced not according to the number of computers sold per year but according to the total number of units installed, or the number of units in stock. This is exactly the situation that exists in the housing industry in Japan, where although the number of housing starts have decreased, the total number of houses in stock is on the rise, generating a demand for house renovations or general repairs and maintenance work.

In the computer industry, there is the same need for experts on software maintenance, with the increase in the number of units installed and the accompanying growth in the number of programs produced. A look at the annual changes in data processing costs (*see* Fig. 21) reveals the increasing emphasis on software, and especially software maintenance, with demand greatly outstripping supply.

An information society relies on software for its continuing prosperity, just as an industrial society recognizes the importance of the production of goods. This propelled MITI officials to establish the Sigma Project, a joint public–private sector research effort aimed at improving software productivity. It is a vast five-year project costing ¥60 billion, a budget that exceeds those of the ULSI and the fifth-generation computer research projects. No detailed information is yet available on the Sigma Project, but its aim is the preparation of standard software units that can be built up or combined—just as machinery can increase productivity with improved interchangeability of parts—and the acceleration of automated manufacturing technology.

Fig. 21: A COMPARISON OF PRICE CHANGES IN HARDWARE AND SOFTWARE

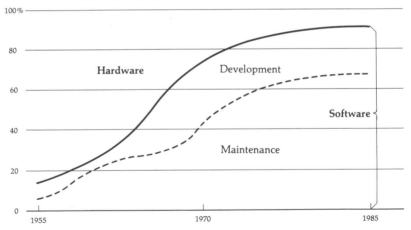

Note: Hardware/software cost ratio: 3 to 7 (1970); 1 to 9 (1985)
Development/maintenance cost ratio: 4 to 6 (1970); 3 to 7 (1985)
Source: B.W. Boehm, *Datamation*, Vol. 19, No. 3.

In Japan the proliferation of standard items of software such as packaged software is still inadequate, so it is necessary to change our basic attitude toward the use of this kind of software. In this sense, our problem is not so much one of technology as one of application. However, in order to increase software production, an improvement in automated program manufacturing technology and a standard program language are required. Languages such as Cobol, Fortran, PL/1 have been popularized (*see* Fig. 22), and high-level ones such as Focus have been developed. With these, users who are not software specialists will be able to prepare programs on their own. In the future, however, as software production increases, demand for conventional programmers will decrease in favor of high-level systems engineers or supertech personnel.

Fig. 22: IMPROVEMENTS IN THE STANDARD OF PROGRAM LANGUAGES

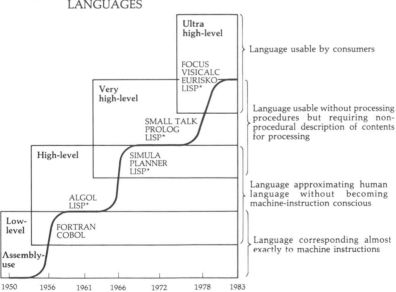

Note: *After undergoing many changes, LISP is now a new language category.
Source: Alan Kay, *Scientific American*, November 1984.

## INTELLECTUAL TECHNOLOGY

When an industrial society reaches its peak—with the full development of machinery capable of turning out all kinds of goods to satisfy consumers—it is time to switch direction. As mentioned in an earlier chapter, the shift from an industrial to an information society occurred when 40 percent of the work force was engaged in information-related jobs and 20 percent in production jobs. The way such a society works is largely dependent on "intellectual technology," or the collection of all sorts of data to be used as aids to planning and forecasting.

Intellectual technology will be required by companies that are planning to launch new businesses and need forecasting, targeting, or planning. Public organizations must be able to choose the best of several programs and be able to assess the merits of each before organizing a new project.

The technology of planning and analysis has advanced so much that it is now possible to forecast accurately the future situation before a project is implemented. A typical success story is the Apollo Program that sent man to the moon. In the early 1960s, President Kennedy stated that man would reach the moon in 1969 at a cost of ¥8 trillion. In the summer of 1969, Apollo 11 landed on the moon as predicted, although the actual cost of the program was ¥9 trillion. However, when the rise in commodity prices are taken into account, the figure first mentioned was exactly on target.

Dr. James E. Webb, head of NASA in those days, stated that the Apollo Program was based on state-of-the-art technology that was collected, improved, and combined into a system. He accredited the success of the Apollo Program to "systems management," which enabled the project to be completed on schedule. In other words, success was the result of intellectual technology.

This feat led people to pay more attention to forecasting and programming. However, it is well to mention here that since forecasts cannot take the unexpected into account, such as a war or an oil crisis, they may not always be accurate as regards economic issues such as oil supply and demand.

There is also the tendency of a forecast, once publicized, to encourage a reverse trend. For instance, the Club of Rome made a forecast that by the year 2000, oil will be scarce and pollution-related deaths will rise. Consequently, energy conservation programs were promoted around the world, resulting in a huge drop in oil consumption, in which antipollution measures taken by various countries also played a part. And with improved environmental control came a longer life expectancy. In this way, although there is nothing incorrect about the forecast itself, it can affect a situation, making it no longer true.

For forecasting, several different methods exist, of which the most representative is the Delphi method. This is a convergence method that is based on sending repeated questionnaires to a group of experts. Another is the simulation method that uses a simulation model to check, for instance, the regional distribution of air pollutants, or to measure plant distribution around an area, or to measure air resistance distribution in cars.

Systems analyses and cost analyses are used by businesses in the United States to choose between two or three alternative plans. These methods were initially developed for strategic planning purposes, such as the selection of air bases for bombers, and are now used by companies for selecting the best traffic systems or the best engine development methods.

Operation research (OR) is a method of planning and selection that is also called the "quantification of common sense." It is used to determine the best overall plan, such as the best location for an oil station, the most efficient transportation system for gasoline, or the most effective procedures for utilizing machinery. OR is used for linear programming (LP) and for PERT (program evaluation and review techniques) that work out daily schedules for construction work and the like.

When we make use of forecasting and planning, we are running into areas of quantifying the unquantifiable in our economy or our society. Physical phenomena or engineering theories have been quantified; however, subjective feelings or views are a different matter. How do we express in figures, say, the comfort of riding in a car, or the pleasing appearance of a certain product?

There are three ways to do this. First, by quantifying human insight, just as market research does for a product about to be launched. Consumers are interviewed and the data collected— the questionnaire approach. For a technical forecast the Delphi method, which relies on a panel of experts to answer a series of questionnaires, is preferred. This enables us to work in areas where no past data have been collected or in the absence of any numerical measurements.

The second method is by quantifying effect through a conversion. Suppose you spend a long time waiting for a bus each morning. The time spent can be converted into a monetary sum, and this method is often used in system analyses.

The third method is by quantifying consciousness, where such emotive words like "pleasant" or "uncomfortable" are converted into figures, a method widely used to assess environmental factors such as traffic noise. There is also a method of scoring by members of a panel, and a utility method, in which the answers to questions prepared for different cases are charted on a graph.

## MANAGEMENT TECHNOLOGY TO SUPPORT GROWTH

The most valuable asset of any company is its employees, who largely determine the fate of the business. It is important to know that they are motivated and work hard. Management technology that enables a company to produce low-cost quality goods is also a feature of intellectual technology. America, once the leader in this field has found itself equaled and surpassed by Japan in many industry sectors. The areas where Japan is strongest are so-called just-in-time management and quality control.

### Just-in-time Management

In auto manufacturing in Japan and the United States, the differences in the cost and productivity indexes are directly due to the management technologies of the two countries. Japanese productivity is centered on just-in-time management, epitomized by the Toyota manufacturing method. In his book *The Toyota System* (Kodansha, 1985), Professor Yasuhiro Kadota of Tsukuba University remarked on it in the following way.

The just-in-time concept stems from making the necessary quantity of goods in the required time. For example, auto unit components needed in the premanufacturing stage must arrive at the assembly line when they are required and in the quantity needed. For this, the *kamban* (signboard) method is used, with the parts needed and their quantities written on a hanging board as they are required.

Supporting the kamban method are the following procedures. 1. Output equalization—most important for minimizing idle time and keeping inventories at a minimum so that there is a balance between inventory and production requirements. 2. Minimum preparation time—the time spent on replacing dyes and jigs is crucial to manufacturing operations, and Toyota has shortened the time required for replacing press molds, which used to take three hours over a decade ago, to five minutes. 3. Work standardization— multifunction workers are needed to handle various kind of machinery in order to synchronize production line operations. 4. Improvement circles—all proposals by workers involved in production are welcomed and discussed at workshop circles at Toyota. This is an essential process for it enables workers to find value in their work and enhances respect among them. 5. Automation—this refers to manned automation, which differs from mechanization, and is used to cut out defective products. An automatic checking system is provided at the end of each manufacturing process, and should any defective items be found, the belt will come to a standstill. This guarantees quality.

When I met Taiichi Ohno, the former vice president of Toyota and the man behind the *kamban* idea, he told me the following anecdote, which still impresses me. A worker came late for work one day only to find that, because there were no surplus workers to fill in for him, the conveyor belt was stopped. That worker never came late again.

*Quality Control*

We all know that quality control (QC) is responsible for the elimination of defects, and the modern method of QC was developed by the American statistician, W. A. Shewhart. Like the histogram (frequency figure) A shown in Figure 23, defective items listed on both sides of the chart are eliminated through inspection. If this inconsistency is abolished, all the products would pass the quality control test as in histogram B. The method of eliminating such defective items through changing the form of distribution is called statistical quality control.

Fig. 23: IMBALANCES IN PRODUCT QUALITY

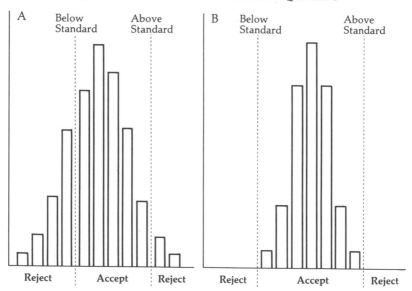

According to Hajime Karatsu, professor at Tokai University, the basic method of statistical quality control can be implemented as follows. One, to catch the factor responsible for product inconsistencies, we must first locate it, and to do this data obtained on the worksite is invaluable. These data will determine the factor or factors responsible for product inconsistencies. This is called the work-process analysis. Two, to confine the factor so that it will not emerge; this is called standardization.

A number of firms have successfully applied quality control to nonmanufacturing departments. This makes sense because in order to eliminate defective goods, we need to keep checks on other processes such as those in the design, purchasing, and personnel departments. This is the total quality control (TCQ) approach, the reason behind the high standards and productivity of Japan's manufacturing industries.

Apart from setting up quality control circles in plants, there are also small on-site QC circles. Most foreign visitors to Japan are impressed by the degree to which workers understand the QC concept, and even young women workers are able to make control charts or histograms. Workers discuss relevant issues in their own time to pursue the reason for defective items. These circles are immensely helpful in raising quality.

The concept of QC was first introduced to Japanese industry in 1951 by W. E. Deming, a statistician. I found that his name is much more familiar to Japanese than to Americans, perhaps one reason for the difference in quality between products of Japan and the United States. In Japan the prestigious annual Deming Award is eagerly sought after by all manufacturers.

## PBD and FAME

At a basic level, improvements in quality and productivity stem from the enthusiasm of the workers who make the products. Small groups and QC circles satisfy the spirit of challenge in Japanese workers, but when it comes to large-scale projects involving the coordination of thousands of manufacturers and suppliers, viz., the Manhattan Project or NASA's artificial satellite program, the Japanese are no match for the Americans.

NASA succeeded in its space development program, the largest in this century, because it gave individual workers a sense of participation and achievement, which contributed to work satisfaction. The way NASA did this was by dividing the whole project into many component parts, of a size that could be handled by a small group. Through the skillful use of package breakdown (PBD), the worker could feel a sense of achievement.

One example of the successful implementation of a long-term R&D program is Texas Instruments, which has a system called OST (for objective, strategy, and tactics). This consists of three stages of action: clarification of business goals, integration of various strategies for their achievement, and a series of tactics. Texas Instruments used OST to successfully develop a front-monitoring nocturvision for the government, a device that enables pilots to fly in complete darkness, guided by a television monitor that displays images.

What impressed me most when I looked at the OST system was the clear job breakdown (see Fig. 24), from objective to strategies to tactics, with research staff appointed for research work at the very start. This made me realize that the division of a system into research, development, technical, and manufacturing departments could work. This method eliminates ambiguities in objective and strategies that stand in the way of innovation, and allows for results achieved through control of technical development.

Texas Instruments asserted that its strategies and tactics were the main support in its development of the nocturvision, and that its inventions and innovations in this were truly astounding. Conversely, I suppose the reason why some R&D projects fail must be due to improper understanding of the strategy, improper evaluation of necessary resources, and improper control over the project.

In such a system, what scares me is the possible disruption in

# Fig. 24: OST SYSTEM BREAKDOWN

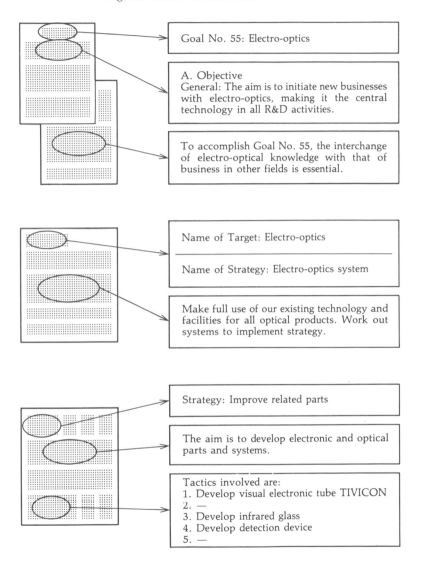

Goal No. 55: Electro-optics

A. Objective
General: The aim is to initiate new businesses with electro-optics, making it the central technology in all R&D activities.

To accomplish Goal No. 55, the interchange of electro-optical knowledge with that of business in other fields is essential.

Name of Target: Electro-optics

Name of Strategy: Electro-optics system

Make full use of our existing technology and facilities for all optical products. Work out systems to implement strategy.

Strategy: Improve related parts

The aim is to develop electronic and optical parts and systems.

Tactics involved are:
1. Develop visual electronic tube TIVICON
2. —
3. Develop infrared glass
4. Develop detection device
5. —

communication between upper and lower echelons when the manager loses control of his department. When I visited NASA headquarters with Masaru Ibuka, honorary chairman of Sony, in 1984, I was astonished at its achievements with huge computers and ultramodern systems technology. In the information systems network, I was especially impressed by what is known as FAME (forecast and appraisals for management evaluation).

The Apollo Program that sent man to the moon was an excellent example of this system. Comprising several million parts, there was complete control of all the processes—from design to manufacturing—scattered over twenty thousand companies throughout the United States. Data were reported to headquarters every minute, and these were handled by computers that not only filed and tabulated them but also analyzed them. By discerning changes in ongoing trends, the computer made forecasts on future values, and if it discovered any minute possibility that these trends may cross the danger line, warnings were immediately sent to controlling officers in the form of forecast information, which were then relayed to the departments concerned so they could make improvements quickly and the spaceship could be completed on schedule.

Japan has not yet mastered the workings of such a system. We have control personnel and technical personnel who are quick to act when they spot something wrong in the manufacturing process, but in a large project the departments concerned are not fully in control.

# 6

# Technological Measures for Internationalization

International relations play a vital part in determining the future of corporations. In the 1970s, Japanese industry had successfully negotiated two turbulent oil crises and had managed to maintain growth, hold unemployment down to 2 percent, and keep a good trade balance. As a result of this success in the face of adversity, the world looked more sternly at Japan. Now, with the dollar exchange rate of ¥140 squeezing Japanese companies into a tight corner, their future prosperity or decline will be largely affected by relations between Japan and the rest of the world.

TRADE FRICTION WITH JAPAN

Immediately before the Bonn Summit of 1985, Japan found itself the object of criticism by the United States for its external trade policy. Japan's trade surplus was growing at an alarming rate, even provoking Prime Minister Nakasone to call on the Japanese people to buy more imported goods. Despite this, American congressional sentiment against Japan grew more hostile, and repeated calls have been made in Congress for trade sanctions against Japan.

Comparing Japan's figures with those of other nations that enjoyed a surplus in 1984, it is clear that Japan led by a long way with a surplus of $36 billion, followed by West Germany with $9 billion, France with $2 billion, and Canada with $250 million. In an attempt to ward off mounting global criticism of Japan, the Japanese government hammered out a market-opening program to increase imports of lumber, electrical and telecommunications equipment, and electronics, and in addition it relaxed its standards and certification system for such items as pharmaceuticals and home electronic appliances. However, it is too simplistic to think that such measures alone will reduce the nation's huge trade surplus. The program is the seventh of its kind; yet the trade surplus continues to grow unabated.

Nevertheless, I feel that this wholesale criticism of Japan is not entirely fair. From the Japanese point of view, there have been substantial changes in the percentage share of its trade deficit with the United States (see Fig. 25), and this figure is falling steadily year by year: from 45.6 percent in 1981, to 44.4. percent in 1982, to 31.2 percent in 1983, and to 29.8 percent in 1984. Even Taiwan, with a population of 18 million, recorded a surplus of $11 billion in its trade with the United States. Yet it is Japan that is singled out for blame.

There is another view prevalent in Japan, which is that Japan is often referred to as a large exporting nation when, in reality, it is a small exporting nation. When its foreign trade is calculated on a per capita basis, it is very small: Japan's per capita trade for 1985 was $1,463 for exports and $1,079 for imports (see Fig. 26), far smaller than West Germany's. Thus, the call for market-opening measures based on trade imbalance does not reflect the actual situation.

Kenichi Ohmae, a senior partner in the international management consulting firm of McKinsey & Co., pointed out that it is the Americans who should be buying more Japanese imports, not the Japanese who should be buying more American goods. His argument was based on sales and production figures for U.S. corporations in Japan, which totaled some $43.9 billion in 1984. This sum represented the total sales of some 300 companies out

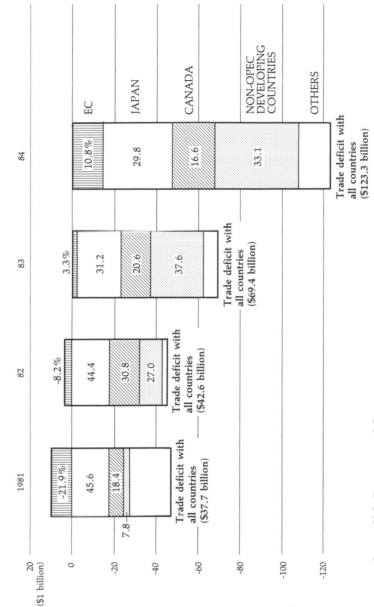

Fig. 25: OTHER COUNTRIES' SHARE IN THE U.S. TRADE DEFICIT

Source: U.S. Department of Commerce.

MEASURES FOR INTERNATIONALIZATION 147

Fig. 26: PER CAPITA TRADE OF MAJOR COUNTRIES (1985)

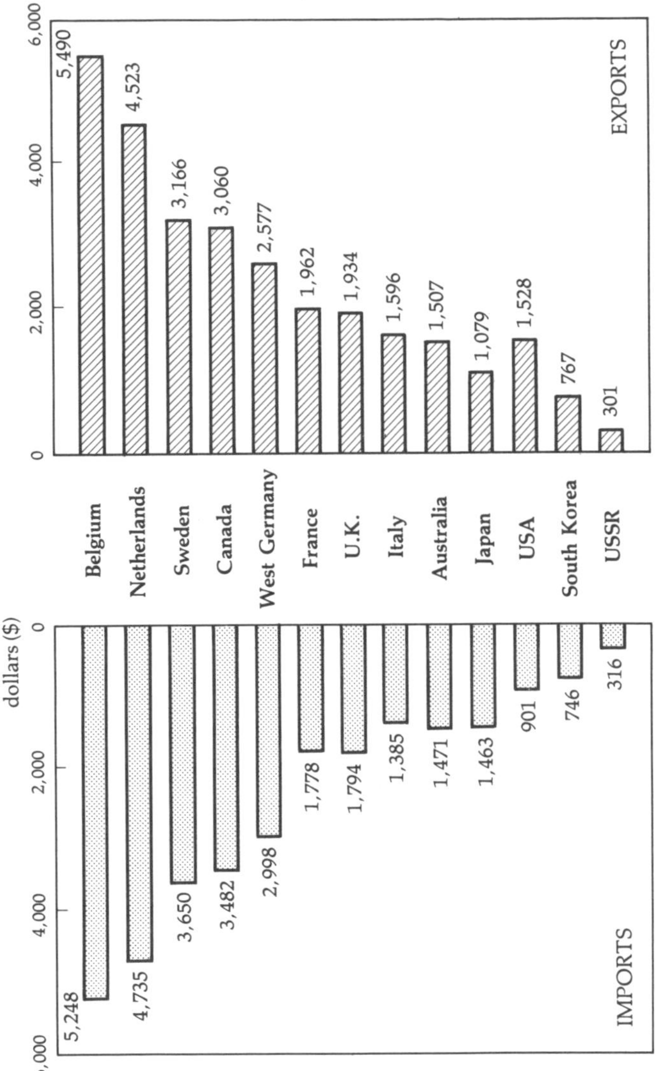

dollars ($)

| | EXPORTS | IMPORTS |
|---|---|---|
| Belgium | 5,490 | 5,248 |
| Netherlands | 4,523 | 4,735 |
| Sweden | 3,166 | 3,650 |
| Canada | 3,060 | 3,482 |
| West Germany | 2,577 | 2,998 |
| France | 1,962 | 1,778 |
| U.K. | 1,934 | 1,794 |
| Italy | 1,596 | 1,385 |
| Australia | 1,507 | 1,471 |
| Japan | 1,079 | 1,463 |
| USA | 1,528 | 901 |
| South Korea | 767 | 746 |
| USSR | 301 | 316 |

of 3,000 American companies operating in Japan. Imports from the United States and goods produced by these companies (which could be described as American goods) were nearly the same as sales and production figures of Japanese products in the United States.

The trade balance figures that are at the center of friction between the two countries are figures for goods that have cleared customs. The Japanese government has made various public relations attempts, including repeated calls on the public to buy U.S. products, to reduce the nation's trade deficit, but the results are far from satisfactory.

*Nihon Keizai Shimbun* had this to say in an editorial on May 17, 1985. "Each Japanese purchased $583 worth of U.S. products last year [*see* Fig. 27], nearly four times the value of American purchases of Japanese goods. In other words, whereas the average Japanese spent approximately 6 percent of his income on U.S.

Fig. 27: CONSUMER SPENDING IN JAPAN AND AMERICA

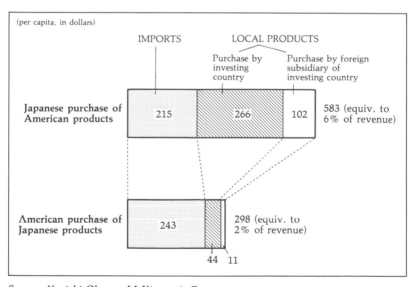

Source: Kenichi Ohmae, McKinsey & Co.

products, the average American spent only 2 percent of his income on Japanese goods during the same year. Paradoxically, shouldn't the Americans be spending an extra $100 to buy Japanese imports?"

However, the situation at present is too tense for this kind of retaliation. The trade dispute has also to be viewed amid the worsening American economy, which is faced with the "twin deficits" of trade and budget. The U.S. economy once had two highs—the high dollar and high interest rates—and two deficits, but although the two highs have been lowered, the two deficits continue to increase.

Will the American trade deficit decrease now that the value of the yen has risen substantially? The answer is no, for although the dollar has dropped significantly vis-à-vis the yen and some European currencies, its value is still high against the currencies of the "four tigers": Hong Kong, Taiwan, Singapore, and South Korea, whose currencies tend to fluctuate with the dollar.

This, combined with the fact that the inner core of American industry has "hollowed out," will insure heavy American dependence on imports in the future. In its trade with Japan, imports of Japanese capital goods, such as office and factory machinery, are still increasing despite the surge in the value of the yen.

A look at the breakdown of U.S.–Japan trade figures shows that the biggest items exported by Japan are machinery—office machinery, VCRs, and communications equipment—where volume is rising, followed by automobiles, steel, precision machinery, and metal products. On the other hand, the top export by the United States are machinery, followed by corn, soybeans, coal, and timber. The nature of the trade between Japan and America is similar to trade between a developed nation and a developing nation.

For these reasons, it is apparent that there will be no reduction in America's trade deficit with Japan even if the dollar remains around the ¥140 level for two or three years. The United

States, suffering from a structural trade deficit as it has to buy capital goods from abroad, desperately needs to restructure its economy.

Considered in this light, its twin deficits of trade and budget are serious ones. In 1975, the U.S. trade balance was in the black, but its financial deficit stood at the not very substantial level of $50 billion. In 1979, its trade balance went into the red for the first time, by only $20 billion to $30 billion, which is not very significant even if the financial deficit of $50 billion was added. However, by 1985, its trade deficit had swelled to $150 billion and its financial deficit to $212.3 billion, and both figures are expected to rise further in 1986. In other words, the United States has changed from a creditor to a debtor nation, and its present situation is like that of a company executive whose private funds are in the red and whose company loans are increasing.

Another reason for the spate of U.S. criticism of Japan derives not from a quantitative factor but from a qualitative one. Long considered the world's leader in high-tech products, Americans are feeling humiliated by the trade deficit in high technology with Japan, and this is a serious problem.

According to a congressional survey, the United States saw its semiconductor trade with Japan plummet to a deficit of $2.2 billion in 1984, its trade in electronic parts registered a deficit of $2.7 billion, and in telecommunications equipment the deficit was $950 million. Thus, the high-tech industries in the United States nosedived from surplus to deficit within a brief period. This reversal of roles is not an easy situation for America to live with, and the high-tech issue will continue to dominate relations between the two countries in the years ahead.

The future information society will be centered around communications networks, and communications technology is now high on the list of high-tech industries. This area, formerly led by the United States, has been invaded by Japan, which is producing a spectacular array of communications equipment that is threatening the very existence of American companies. And these companies are most uncomfortable with the situation.

If you look at the trends in the export of communications equipment to the United States (*see* Fig. 28), Japanese exports shot up to ¥259.4 billion in 1984, or a massive 6.5 fold increase over the ¥39.6 billion recorded in 1979. American exports of communications equipment to Japan failed to keep up, rising from ¥5.4 billion in 1979 to ¥22.4 billion in 1984. Americans cannot believe they were so easily surpassed by the Japanese in the high-tech field; therefore, they argue, there must be something fishy, and conclude that Japan's import restrictions are to blame. However, since actual exports of communications equipment from Japan include a number of items, such as telephones, that are not high-tech products, the situation is less pessimistic than it appears. Still, the statistics do not make Americans feel any easier, and I can understand why the United States keeps up its pressure on Japan, demanding the abolition of restrictions on imports.

Fig. 28: U.S.–JAPAN TRADE IN COMMUNICATIONS EQUIPMENT

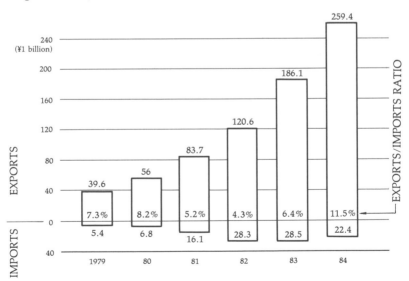

*The Semiconductor Industry in Japan and the United States*

It was in 1980 that Japan first began exporting more ICs than it was importing from the United States, and by 1984 Japan was showing a ¥208.6 billion surplus in this trade. The following year saw a slackening off in semiconductor trade, but the trade gap between the two countries remained large.

It is worth noting that the average price of an IC exported by Japan was three times higher than one imported from America for the simple reason that Japan was exporting higher-grade products, such as 256K DRAMs, while the United States was exporting cheaper TTL-type logic circuits. In the case of the 256K DRAMs, Japanese products account for over 90 percent of the world market, making Japan the chief source for this type of IC. Moving down one rank, to 64K DRAMs, we see that Japan holds nearly 60 percent of the world market.

How do Japanese products compare with American products overall? In many respects, American products are superior, especially in their excellent software, but when it comes to the performance of computers, Japanese computers are able to hold their own, even in the new supercomputers field. American technology may have lost its edge in many areas, yet in microprocessors, it still retains the lead.

A general comment about Japan heard abroad is that because Japan leads in the production of metal oxide semiconductors (MOS), its semiconductor technology is superior to that of the United States, but the truth is that the United States cannot produce electronic goods without supplies of Japanese-made parts. Even IBM personal computers assembled in the United States have a 73 percent cost reliance ($800 per unit) on imported parts. In addition, Japanese suppliers produce half the semiconductors and units, such as graphic printers, keyboards, and power supplies, while American companies only produce cases, disk drives, and do the assembling.

A comprehensive bilateral agreement on the semiconductor

trade was reached in July 1986, when it was decided to implement a system whereby the government would supervise prices to prevent the dumping of Japanese semiconductors in America. This system would also cover Japanese exports to "third" countries, while Japan would step up efforts to help American semiconductors gain greater access into the Japanese market. If the above provisions are fulfilled, the American government will drop its case against imports of Japanese 256K DRAMs and EEPROMs (electronic erasing, rewriting capabilities), taken up in accordance with Section 301 of the U.S. Trade Act of 1974.

An interesting response to this is the EC's claim with GATT (General Agreement on Tariffs and Trade) that imported ICs have become too costly and that it is outrageous for prices to be decided upon by the United States and Japan.

The dependence of American industries on Japan for high-tech machinery parts is growing, and it underlines the general weakness in American high-tech industries. In the automobile industry, for instance, where many Japanese companies have formed joint ventures with American companies, General Motors and Toyota, Chrysler and Mitsubishi, Ford and Mazda, a phenomenon has been observed where studies in production processes have been turned over to the Japanese side. In each of these cases, while the assembly work is done in the United States, the rights to plant design and project engineering are entrusted to the Japanese companies. In the Chrysler–Mitsubishi contract, engines, transmissions, and accelerators are to be imported from Japan.

This trend is not without danger for the United States. As Japanese companies are entrusted with more and more value-added products, there will be less opportunities for technicians in the United States to design their own products and make improvements in the production process. Therefore, a situation could develop in which the United States retains only the first and last links in the chain covering basic research, production, and marketing.

This phenomenon is observed in other fields, too. Westinghouse closed its Braun TV picture tube factory in New York State ten years ago because it was losing out to competition from Japanese tube makers. Now this same factory will be reopened as part of a joint venture with Toshiba, and it is Toshiba that will have to handle the technology because Westinghouse technicians have not done this sort of work for ten years.

In automobiles sold in the United States, there is a growing reliance on Japanese-made engines. This category of cars include American-made cars with Japanese engines, foreign (made in Korea) cars with Japanese engines, Japanese cars made in America, and cars imported from Japan. According to the statistics, about half the American-made cars will have Japanese-made engines and transmissions by 1990. This tendency, where the most technology-intensive parts of American-made cars (engines and transmissions) will be made in Japan, is expected to prevail in the field of car electronics as well.

## Japan and Newly Industrialized Countries

There is another source of trade friction involving Japan, and it is one that will continue to smolder over a long period of time. It concerns the issue of technological transfers involving NICs (newly industrialized countries) and developing countries. I first heard about the issue when I was invited to South Korea by Pohan Steel to lecture at the International Society of Materials.

Pohan Steel completed the first phase of its project with the technical cooperation of the Japanese, and it now produces 10 million tons of steel annually. However, since supply cannot keep up with the brisk demand, Pohan is considering going ahead with the second phase of construction, which will raise production to 20 million tons annually, large enough to be ranked with Japan's major steel producers.

However, when Pohan approached the same Japanese steel company to help it, the Japanese company refused, citing the possibility of exports of Korean steel to Japan as a reason. This sounds a bit selfish to me. Japan itself got the technology, as well as the technological expertise, from America to build its industrial base and today Japan is exporting high-tech products to America. Why does Japan refuse to help Korea when the latter is trying to follow Japan's example.

At the moment, when criticism of Japan is heard worldwide, accompanied by accusations of unfair trade practices, such cases only throw more evidence of Japan's bad behavior into the light. It was some time ago that I met a leading Japanese entrepreneur, well known in the shipbuilding industry for his business philosophy. He told me that there was no difference in the quality of Korean and Japanese sheet steel, and the Korean steel costs less. However, he said he would not import it because of Japanese distributors' suspicions of Korean imports. Such attitudes, as well as the refusal to give technical assistance, are expected to grow more entrenched as the years go by, and it is important for the Japanese to act now before they do more damage to this country's industry.

Pohan Steel has now abandoned hopes of technical assistance from Japan, and instead has tied up with U.S. Corp., the largest American steelworks. In this way Korea will cut its economic ties with Japan and move toward a closer relationship with America, which will be dangerous for Japan unless it gives more thought to its attitude in future. For unlike the U.S.–Japan trade relationship, where the United States is far more powerful and where friction between the two may ease off at a certain level, Japan's relationship with NICs, including Korea, is expected to worsen in the coming years.

## THE LEVEL OF JAPANESE TECHNOLOGY

What are the characteristics of Japanese technology when viewed from an international angle and examined at each individual step of the process: namely, research, development, and production? At which level does Japanese technology slot into world technology as a whole? Japanese products are known worldwide as good copies of foreign products; yet some say that the finished products should be considered for what they are, without scientific research playing any part.

Therefore, I would like to scrutinize the strengths and weaknesses of Japanese technology at each stage, starting with basic research. The result of research is an invention, and the invention may even win academic acclaim or a special award. The next stage is development. William Shockley may have invented the transistor, but it was Sony that made the most use out of it with its transistor radio. In other words, development refers to the stage where the result of research is incorporated into an actual product. After this comes the final stage of production, and typical examples are automobiles and steel, which require the technology of producing products at low cost and in high quantities, i.e., mass-production technology.

The view generally held about Japanese technology is that Japan tends to get stronger as it moves into the later stages. It is weak in invention, relatively good at development, but best at mass-production and commercialization.

Japan's basic shortcoming in research stems from its weakness in creativity, a view that is shared by the Japanese themselves. Evidence to support this claim is shown in Figure 29, on "Changes in Japan's Trade in Technology" (1986 White Paper on Science and Technology), where Japan's deficit in technology trade underlines its weakness in the stage of research. Technology trade refers to the payment, and receipt, of money for patents, utility models, or technical know-how. For instance, if a Japanese manufacturer uses a U.S. patent for his products, he has to pay a patent fee to the patent owner. This is a technological import. In 1972, Japan's technology imports amounted to ¥174 billion, against ¥42 billion in exports; in 1985, imports totaled ¥281 billion against ¥278 billion in exports. Although Japan has chalked up surpluses in its manufactured goods trade balance, it suffers from a deficit in technology trade. Payments for technology such as patents stem from differences in the research stage in Japan and

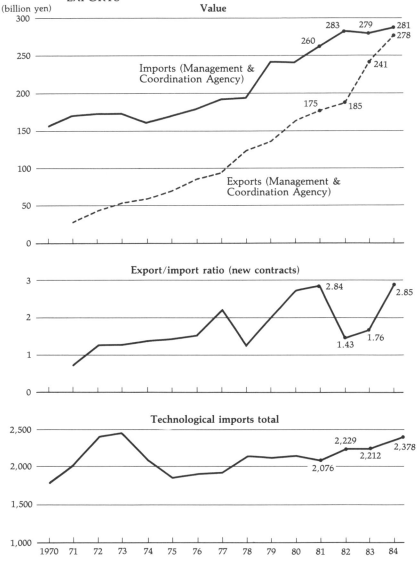

Fig. 29: CHANGES IN JAPAN'S TECHNOLOGICAL IMPORTS AND EXPORTS

(billion yen)

**Value**

Imports (Management & Coordination Agency)

Exports (Management & Coordination Agency)

**Export/import ratio (new contracts)**

**Technological imports total**

Source: Science and Technology Agency White Paper, 1986.

other countries, and Japan's deficit here is regarded as proof that it is poor at the research level.

Further analysis of the figures shows, however, that the total sum represents patents that were imported in the past and distant past. If the figure for newly contracted technology trade for the past year (payments and receipts effected at the contractual time) is reviewed, a different picture emerges. Japan's balance has been in the black since 1972, when its technology exports exceeded its imports at a rate of 1.26 times. In other words, the level of Japanese technology in the research stage is not as hopeless as it is made out to be. However, it is still a fact that Japan's overall technology trade is in the red when contracts signed in the past are taken into account.

Another proof of the claim that Japan is weak at the research level is its share of Nobel Prize winners: four in Japan and over one hundred in the United States. This really spells out the difference between the two countries. Thus, it is a fact that Japan lags behind the United States and Europe in the area of basic research, especially when military-related technology is included, where basic research is vital.

As mentioned earlier, what is making both the United States and Europe nervous is Japan's speed in catching up with them in the technological race. Japan is like a runner in a marathon who is so far behind that nobody notices him until he is suddenly just behind the winner, in this case America. Such instances are becoming more common today, and Americans and Europeans are becoming increasingly wary of Japan.

In the area of basic research, Figure 30 shows changes in the numbers of papers published at ISSCC by country. ISSCC, or the International Solid-State Circuit Conference, is the world's most authoritative conference for semiconductor-related research, and reports presented in the conference are selected only after tough screening. In 1975, the total number of papers published was 78, including 5 from Japan, 17 from other countries, and 56 from the United States, or 70 percent of the total. In 1985,

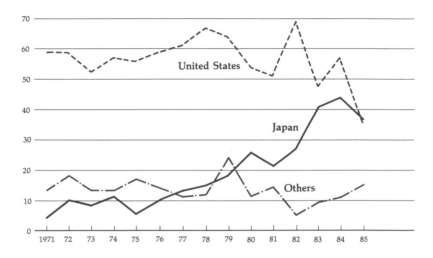

however, U.S. papers numbered 35, and Japanese papers 37, or more than 40 percent of the total. Here, too, the trend is reversing in Japan's favor.

Japan can be said to have caught up with the United States in research on solid-state circuits, the basis of electronics. As a well-known professor of computers at Tokyo University once told me, it used to be that when a researcher in electronics wanted to take up a new subject for study, his superior would ask him if work was being done on it also in the United States. If it was, the superior gave his consent to go ahead. Today, however, American professors would first ask researchers if work was being done on it in Japan. If it is, then they are allowed to go ahead. In the field of electronics, American researchers have set a goal of working on what is being researched in Japan, and there are some areas of basic research being done in Japan which America respects greatly.

In per-capita research spending, "Changes in Research Expenditure" (see Fig. 31) show that total research expenditure for 1984 amounted to ¥23.1 trillion for the United States, ¥7.7 trillion for the Soviet Union, ¥7.9 trillion for Japan, and ¥4.1 trillion for West Germany. It was only in 1979 that Japan overtook West Germany to rank third, but, despite this, Japan's investment only accounts for a little over one-third of that of the United States.

These figures, however, are deceptive for, in the case of the United States, they include military research expenditure, which amounts to approximately half the U.S. total. The United States is reputed to be spending some ¥200 trillion on the SDI project and several trillions of yen on the development of missiles, whereas Japan only appropriates ¥60 billion to ¥70 billion on so-called national defense research. Considering that a private business in Japan will invest over ¥120 billion on research, national defense research expenditure is very low and only amounts to half that sum.

In short, expenses that go to private R&D projects amount to ¥12 trillion for the United States, compared with ¥6.1 trillion for Japan. In terms of per capita spending, Japan's research expenses nearly equal those of the United States. Thus, there is no truth in the claim made by foreign governments that Japan's research spending is too small. It may be small when compared with the government budget, but it stands on a par with the United States' spending on private sector research.

In research expenditure it is not the amount that is spent that is important but what the money is spent on. An examination will reveal the ineffectual utilization of government funds on research, as well as the inefficiency of government projects that are devouring taxpayers' money in Japan.

The ratio of organizations contributing to and organizations using research funds in major countries (see Fig. 32) shows that, in the United States, about half the research funds come from the government. However, of that sum, 70 percent is given to private research institutions. It is often mistakenly thought that

## Fig. 31: CHANGES IN R&D EXPENDITURE OF MAJOR COUNTRIES

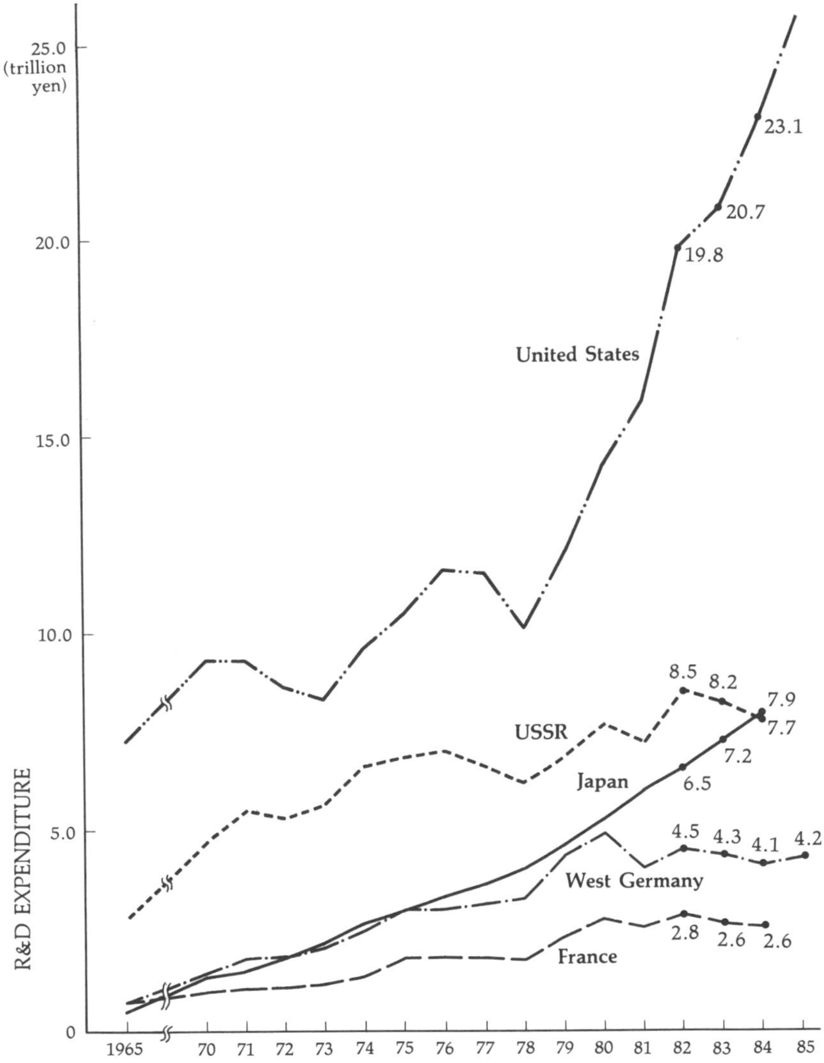

Note: The figures denote total expenditures on natural, human, and social sciences.

Source: Science and Technology Agency White Paper, 1986.

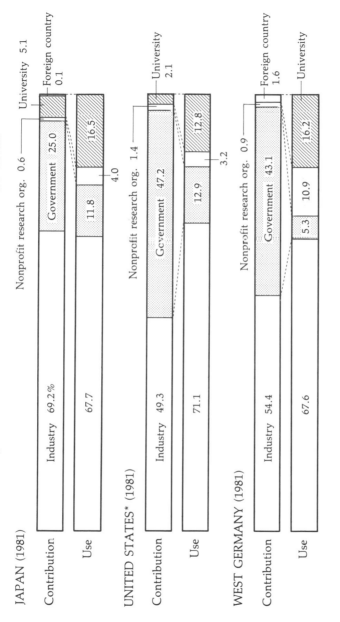

Fig. 32: RATIO OF R&D CONTRIBUTORS TO R&D USERS

JAPAN (1981)

Nonprofit research org. 0.6

University 5.1

Contribution — Industry 69.2% — Government 25.0 — University 5.1 — Foreign country 0.1

Use — 67.7 — 11.8 — 4.0 — 16.5

UNITED STATES* (1981)

Nonprofit research org. 1.4

University 2.1

Contribution — Industry 49.3 — Government 47.2 — University 2.1

Use — 71.1 — 12.9 — 3.2 — 12.8

WEST GERMANY (1981)

Nonprofit research org. 0.9

Foreign country 1.6

Contribution — Industry 54.4 — Government 43.1 — Foreign country 1.6

Use — 67.6 — 5.3 — 10.9 — University 16.2

Note: *Denotes estimates. Figures for countries other than Japan and West Germany include expenditures on cultural and social sciences.

Source: Science and Technology Agency.

MEASURES FOR INTERNATIONALIZATION   163

the government supplies the major funds for R&D research in America, but, in fact, this is done by private business. In Japan, the situation is just the reverse; it is private businesses that bear 70 percent of R&D costs, with the government contributing the remaining 30 percent. The same is true of the user ratio, with the government share mostly spread among government-affiliated research departments and universities. Looked at in another way, government funds are distributed to government institutions notorious for their lack of motivation, pulling Japan behind in basic research.

Government research funds come from taxes and, unlike private research money, are not honestly earned by hard work. Moreover, government researchers and university professors, the beneficiaries, do not have to show any worthwhile work since they are protected by the lifetime employment system. Neither will their organizations go bankrupt if they work at half-mast. The perpetuation of such a system is lowering the standards of basic research in Japan, and with money automatically pouring into such channels, it is small wonder that research suffers as a result.

Rather, government funds for research should be awarded to the more efficient private research institutions, more in keeping with the situation in the United States. A *Sankei Shimbun* survey once compared the efficiency of fund use between private and government R&D investments, and found that the recovery rate of government R&D investment totaled under one-twentieth that of private R&D investment.

This slackness must be changed if the level of basic research is to be raised in Japan. There are three ways of doing this: 1. introduce a performance rating in national research institutions and university research departments that will allow for the firing of personnel or the disbanding of organizations that fail; 2. give government funds to private research institutions; and 3. replace government research personnel with more aggressive researchers from private organizations to promote exchanges of staff. I recall a reporter from a weekly magazine once calling me up to ask for my comment regarding the news that a chief researcher at a government institute had opted to join a private institution. This simple event made news in Japan just because this sort of exchange is almost without precedent in this country.

Jun'ichi Nishizawa is a professor at Tohoku University and the director of its Semiconductor Research Institute. He is also a trailblazer in his field of semiconductors, lasers, and optical fibers, was nominated for the Nobel Prize in 1984, and made the cover of *Electronics* magazine of the United States as Mr. Electronics. He told me of the importance of both a highly charged atmosphere and the concentration of energy in a research laboratory. Without such tension, he said, research is not possible.

Another reason for Japan's weakness in basic research is a national character trait that shuts out anyone with a marked individuality in favor of a blander type of person. This type of character is well suited for manufacturing but not for research jobs. Such cultural differences also affect outlook, as the book, *The Wisdom of Japan and the Wisdom of Europe*, by Hisako Matsubara (Mikasa Shobo, 1985) makes clear. In it she observes that a man of culture in the United Kingdom is a man who is steeped in the Greek classics, who enjoys reading philosophy, and who is a devotee of classical music. A man who is up to the minute in new technology is not considered cultured, but a man who stands in front of a new machine looking perplexed is.

These cultural differences are also reflected in the corporate world, which in the United Kingdom tends to hold the use of office computers in contempt. In Japan, on the other hand, even presidents and senior executives are attending computer classes in order to tackle new office equipment. Thus, whereas the Japanese attach supreme importance to production, the British look down on it. (Prime Minister Margaret Thatcher was amazed to learn of the number of university graduates at a Nissan plant she was visiting.) In the United Kingdom, however, a research position is considered prestigious, perhaps the reason for the number of Nobel Prize winners in that country and its strength in the field of research. Japan would do well to divert some of the attention it places on production, a goal it has succeeded through the elimination of defective products, and focus some of it on research.

## THE IMPORTANCE OF THE DEVELOPMENT STAGE

Microelectronics started off with the invention of the transistor by William Shockley, and its application in the transistor radio was achieved by Sony. Then the integrated circuit was invented, and again it was Japan that triumphed in its application. Such cases, where Japan broke through in the stage of development, are common.

The growth of the Japanese IC industry (*see* Fig. 33) shows that IC trade between Japan and the United States continued with a deficit of ¥32.2 billion for Japan until 1979. The following year Japan chalked up a surplus close to ¥2.8 billion, in 1981 some ¥700 million, in 1982 some ¥33.2 billion, in 1983 some ¥76.7 billion, in 1984 some ¥208.6 billion, in 1985 some ¥94.2 billion, in 1986 some ¥53.8 billion. ICs, although "born" in the United Kingdom, were "raised" by Japan to stand on their own feet, and in this way Japan can be compared to a foster parent.

On a visit to the United States some ten years ago, I heard the following anecdote. Whenever a new invention is publicized in Europe, the Soviets are the first to react, saying, "We made the same invention five years ago." The Americans will then say, "Let's industrialize it for mass-production in five or six years' time." And to everyone's surprise, the Japanese will come up with the mass-produced products on the market in three years.

The Japanese are skilled at rapid adaption of a new invention for mass-production, a tendency that irritates Americans, who charge that "Japan commercializes American inventions and then floods our market with them." America cannot bear the idea of anyone getting a free ride at the expense of someone else.

Fig. 33: IC TRADE BETWEEN JAPAN AND THE UNITED STATES

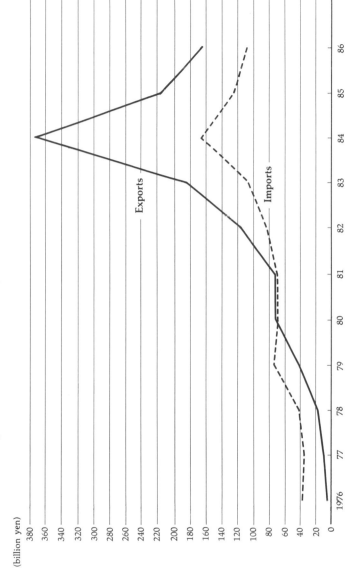

(billion yen)

Exports

Imports

Source: Customs clearance statistics, Ministry of Finance.

However, developing a new product, or putting an invention into practical use is not as easy as it sounds. The "foster parent" has to go through greater hardships than the real parent. Most parents in the United States and Europe give birth to new inventions only to abandon them, and these are picked up and adapted by the foster parent, Japan. In the Edo period (1603–1868), there was a case where the real parents and the foster parents of a child went to court, and the famous magistrate, Ooka Echizen-no-Kami, ruled that the parents who raised the child went through greater difficulties and should have custody of the child.

I myself have had the experience of "fostering" an invention, and it supports this magistrate's words admirably. When I was a graduate student at Tokyo University in 1946, I invented an MT magnet, a high-quality magnet without nickel and cobalt. In 1950, I succeeded in developing this magnet, and later I sold the technology to Indiana Steel Corp. of the United States for about ¥200 million (in current terms). At the same time I built a manufacturing plant in Japan to mass-produce the magnets in compliance with the Japan Industrial Standard (JIS). When nickel and cobalt were available in later years, I closed down the plant in 1964 and sold everything to Mitsubishi Steel Manufacturing. Thus, I experienced firsthand all the stages from invention to development to mass-production (in addition to meeting JIS specifications), plus exporting technology to the United States and shutting down the plant, and of the three stages—research, development, and mass-production—the greatest difficulties were in the stage of development.

Invention is largely influenced by luck, and if you look at the inventions of Tokushichi Mishima, of MK Steel fame and my teacher, or those of Reona Esaki, famed for Esaki diodes, or of William Shockley, you will certainly come across the words "by chance." However, this element of luck or chance is not there in the second stage of development, which is fraught with hardships.

To return to the subject of MT magnets, when Tokyo Keiki,

a leading nautical and flight instruments manufacturer, heard that an American company had inquired about purchasing the patent for the magnet, it quickly took over my invention for industrialization in Japan. Japanese have the habit of not giving credit to anything unless Americans rate it highly.

I was a part-time lecturer at the university, but I joined the company and built a test plant, making the rounds of the clientele personally to present the test-manufactured samples. However, the client companies were in no hurry to place orders. Some employees in the materials department were openly scornful, quite understandably, since it was their heads that would roll if the product failed.

The MT magnets were then used for permanent magnet generators for Honda's motorcycles and Osaki Electric's wattmeters, so we had to take great care over their production. We test-produced samples over and over again, and although we were successful in the laboratory, we had a pile of defective products that had irregular magnetism. With the delivery dates drawing near, we often worked through the night and were surprised to see the dawn. This situation went on for five years before our efforts finally paid off.

Although the development stage is so fraught with hardships, it is crucial to the process of new product industrialization, a fact substantiated by Sony and Honda, two companies that are strong in this stage and have experienced very rapid growth as a result.

Even Thomas Edison, the king of inventors and remembered chiefly for his invention of an incandescent electric bulb, worked on the development stage. The electric bulb was not Edison's invention, but what he did achieve and gained fame for was a bulb that did not burn out. In order to do this, Edison made filaments out of thousands of kinds of materials, and what eventually worked for him was a filament made from the burned carbons of a bamboo grown in Kyoto, Japan. In this way, Edison played the role of intermediary between invention and mass-production.

At the same time, in England, Joseph Swan also developed an

electric bulb using carbon for the filaments, and he sued Edison over the bulb patent. When the case was brought to trial, the judge ruled that, although the same material was used for the filaments, Edison's carbon filament was thin, while Swan's was thick. Judge Fry thus put an end to the dispute on the grounds of the thickness of the carbon used.

A company that copies a product industrialized by the pioneer company is a second-rung company. However, a company that attempts to develop a practical product from an abandoned invention is placed between front runner and runner-up, in a position I call the 1.5th place. Winning a competition from this position is very attractive, and my advice is for businesses to place themselves in the 1.5th position.

Even if you have five hundred researchers working for you, there are several thousand times that many researchers in the world. This also means that there must be thousands of inventions that have failed to bear fruit. Consequently, acquiring one of these projects for industrialization makes for a likely operation strategy. Sony, Honda, Mazda, Ishikawajima-Harima Heavy Industries, and Kyocera are all companies that have succeeded with this strategy.

We have mentioned how William Shockley invented the transistor, how Regency Corp. test-manufactured it, and how Sony used it in its transistor radio. The same situation is seen as regards compact discs, or CDs. Already the hottest-selling electronic audio appliance, a CD works by means of a laser beam, which writes and reads out information, its mechanism characterized by noncontact writing and reading of digital signals. This results in clear, pure sound. At the same time, it has a large storage capacity, able to hold the entire "Ninth Symphony" by Beethoven, which used to take up three sides of an LP record.

CD technology was the invention of Philips, and once again it was Sony that industrialized it. When the CD player first appeared, sales were sluggish because it was expensive and very few discs were then available. Now the cost of the player is down to ¥50,000 and it is supported by a large choice of software. However, the director of Philips once told me that Philips cannot produce CDs without using Sony's patents.

This illustrates the importance of the 1.5th position, which is likened to the role of foster parent. To foster a product that is still in the simple idea stage and put that into practical use is the basis of innovation, as well as the basic strategy that determines the outcome of a company. In this way, Regency, NSU, and Philips all lost the honor of putting a new product on the market to Sony.

## AN ANALYSIS OF JAPAN'S STRENGTH IN PRODUCTION

A survey conducted jointly by *Nihon Keizai Shimbun* (Jan. 1, 1985) and BHA Corp. of the United States attempted to compare the technological strengths of Japan, the United States, and Europe (*see* Fig. 34). It was sent to some three hundred managers in the above countries, asking them to list the country they believed strongest in certain technological segments. Some 81 percent of those polled cited Japan as the leader in manufacturing technology in 1985, with 68 percent believing that Japan will continue to lead in the year 2000. Another 17 percent cited the United States as the leader in manufacturing technology in 1985, with 29 percent believing this will still be true in 2000. Thus, the disparity between Japan and the United States in manufacturing technology is foreseen as being reduced by the year 2000.

In electronic parts, 49 said that Japan was the leader in 1985, with 64 percent believing this will still be true in 2000. In computer technology, 6 percent thought Japan to be strongest in 1985, rising to 21 percent in the year 2000. In artificial intelligence, 13 percent found Japan strongest in 1985, the figure rising to 26 percent in the year 2000. At the same time, the survey showed that only a small number of those polled thought Japanese technology superior in software, communications, new materials, and biotechnology.

However, when it comes to manufacturing technology, there

Fig. 34: THE TECHNOLOGICAL MIGHT OF JAPAN, THE U.S., AND EUROPE

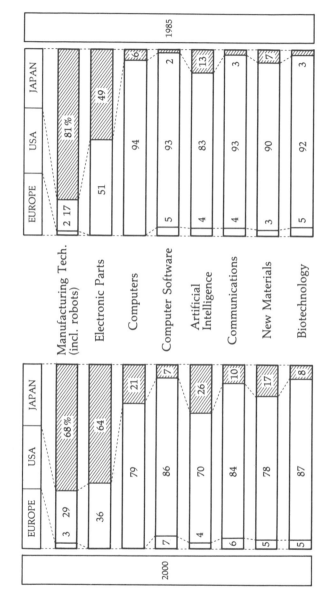

Note: Result of a questionnaire survey conducted by *Nihon Keizai Shimbun* and BHA Corp. of the U.S. The survey covered 300 business managers in Japan, the U.S. and Europe, asking them to name the region they believed best in the respective fields.

Source: *Nikkei Sangyo Shimbun*, January 1, 1985.

is no doubt that Japan leads the rest of the world. It is able to do this with its highly efficient two-tiered production processes, that of process automation and factory automation. Process automation is best represented by the steel, chemical, and oil refining industries, the main pillars of Japan's economy, where heavy investment characterizes the manufacturing plants. Factory automation refers to the assembly operations in manufacturing plants.

There are three reasons behind Japan's strength in manufacturing that are still valid today. First, Japanese are very quick when it comes to introducing new machinery. When I visited the United States some ten years ago, I was surprised to see open-hearth furnaces at Armco Steel. In Japan these furnaces have all been replaced by converters, which were invented by Australia but put into practical use by Japan. When I asked why Armco did not use converters, an official explained that they were not yet through with the depreciation of open-hearth furnaces. The Japanese did not hesitate to dispose of an out-of-date facility even if it was only five or six years old.

The tendency in Japan to pounce on anything new is due largely to the presence of engineers on the plant who know which processes should be streamlined. Japanese factory workers are also more flexible when it comes to changes. West German factories, for instance, still rely on respected master craftsmen, who understandably have little interest in new technology but whose reputation is valued by foremen, engineers, and even technologists alike. If you do not know what processes in your plant are outdated, you won't know what new processes should be installed. This situation is found in all European countries.

The second reason behind Japan's strength in manufacturing is the speed with which the Japanese responded to economies of scale. For instance, seven or eight of the ten largest blast furnaces, with capacities of five thousand cubic meters or over, were in service in Japan when the first oil crisis struck in 1973. The only other country that operated blast furnaces of this size was the

Soviet Union—no other countries had taken advantage of economies of scale and rebuilt their old blast furnaces.

Lastly, the swift introduction of computers in Japanese factories, as well as the excellent uses made of them, is also responsible for Japan's lead in manufacturing. This may be due to the Japanese flair for science and math, already well known after several achievement tests given to schoolchildren all over the world. (In a science test for ninth graders, Japan obtained a score of 73 points, Hungary 68, Australia 58, West Germany 55, and the United States 51. Similar results were obtained in math tests for ninth graders.)

An American report on the cost advantage in the manufacture of Japanese compact cars was prepared by the Secretary of Transport for presentation to Congress in an effort to win financial support for Chrysler, and included data that compared the unit production costs of Japanese and American cars (May 1982). In terms of technology, at that time Japan held the edge over the United States by $73. However, the key to the Japanese advantage over the United States was its management technology, where Japan led by the sum of $1,398 in production costs.

When the figure was broken down, the largest cost advantage of Japanese cars was in the just-in-time management system, contributing $550, followed by quality control, amounting to $329, and other production improvements totaling $478. Thus, the real strength of the Japanese auto industry lies not in its technology but in its management systems, and by far the greatest contribution is made by the just-in-time delivery system of parts and components devised by Toyota.

In this connection, it should be pointed out that, first, it is the small and medium-sized companies that uphold the just-in-time system of delivery. As a race the Japanese are of average ability; in baseball terms, there are no four hundred hitters but two hundred and eighty hitters are quite commonplace. No large company can turn out quality products if the small and medium companies, which are its suppliers, have a low technological level.

Second, the use of robots and other high technology has played a great part in improving Japanese productivity. At present 67 percent to 70 percent of the world's robots are used in Japan, and Japanese small and medium-sized companies that use robots for design work outnumber their American counterparts. In addition, the use of NC machine tools is higher here than in the United States.

Third, quality control (QC) activities are adopted with enthusiasm in Japan, with the full participation of all employees. Even when I was factory manager at Mitsubishi Steel, QC circles were already in existence, with women workers drawing up P charts to check on defective products. Many companies have small groups of five or six workers who get together after working hours to discuss QC improvements.

The situation in the United States is exactly the reverse of that in Japan, i.e., there is a disparity in the level of worker- ability in America. Moreover, high technology is heavily oriented toward the military, with only a slight dispersal of such technologists in private businesses.

In the United States, the attitude of managers shows up another difference between the two countries. American managers tend to be the elite, with MBAs tucked under their arms, and their management approach and business philosophy are very different from those of their Japanese counterparts. American managers are rated by quarterly stock quotations and by quarterly profits, and unless they have a good showing in both, they are out. Thus, American companies are geared to short-term strategies, and no American manager will tackle a long-term strategy that may involve years of being in the red.

There is a rating system in American business management known as the portfolio system, where a chart shows the relationship between growth and profit as the axes of abscissa and ordinates, respectively. In this way, products with high growth potential and high profits are cleared for continued production, while those with slow growth and low profits are abandoned.

This may work well in the United States, but it hinders the development of products in the long term. It is this view that American managers are lacking in.

Businesses that have several MBA managers in their employ are especially at a disadvantage since these managers in control of day-to-day operations will shun innovation, which carries a certain amount of risk. As they are judged on their quarterly earnings, they stick to the profit-first principle, without realizing that profit is the outcome, not the objective, of a business strategy.

The cutthroat competition in Japan, in a literal sense as well, especially in the auto industry, keeps every company on its toes. For example, there are ten auto manufacturing companies in Japan, against four in the United States and two or three in each major European country. Japanese auto companies are strong worldwide because they have been honed on the intensely competitive climate at home. It is competition that has helped them improve their products as well as grow stronger.

It is the same in the Japanese computer industry. There are not many companies manufacturing mainframes overseas because IBM is too large for them to tackle. In Japan there used to be six mainframe manufacturers and now there are three, all competing fiercely with each other. In the Japanese market, Fujitsu is ranked first, followed by NEC and IBM in that order. Without such competition, the Japanese computer industry would not be as strong as it is today. Take the case of the defunct Unidata, a joint computer manufacturing effort between Cii of France, Siemens of West Germany, and Philips of the Netherlands. When it was first set up, Unidata was ready to take on the world, with its attitude of "let's see what IBM will do now." In two or three years, it went under because it had no competition.

Despite these successes, Japanese business management is not without its faults and weaknesses. Take manufacturing technology, for instance. The pursuit of economies of scale have resulted in manufacturers flooding overseas markets with their goods whenever there is a recession in Japan. The just-in-time delivery system of parts can be seen as an attempt by big business to subjugate small and medium-sized companies, which should be more like the venture businesses of the United States, independent and creative. Japanese business management also tends to place a heavy workload on factory workers, forcing them to give up their free time for QC and other circle activities after hours.

In short, although a lot of misunderstanding about Japan exists, most of the criticism directed at Japan is right, and there are a number of reforms that are necessary in Japanese business operations.

## COMMENTS ON FOREIGN MISUNDERSTANDING OF JAPAN

The hard-working Japanese is often the butt of foreign criticism. What is it that motivates him is also a question often asked of Japanese visitors abroad. To answer this, Shichihei Yamamoto, the famous thinker, quoted the Zen priest, Shozo Suzuki.

Shozo Suzuki lived during the turbulent years of transition [the Edo period was begun in 1603], being born in 1579, and until his death at the age of seventy-seven, he remained an extraordinary priest of the Zen sect.

Foreigners tend to think of Zen as something subtle and profound, regarding it as a "mystery" of the Orient. At the same time, they brand the Japanese as economic animals. When asked about Zen by foreigners, I always quote Suzuki's saying, not without some cynicism, that to the Japanese work is not an economic act but an ascetic practice, just as a Zen priest believes there is no work other than the practice of Buddhism. The work of a salaried man also represents the practice of Buddhism; in fact, all types of work are ultimately regarded as the practice of Buddhism. A manufacturer produces things that benefit the world in an effort to emulate Buddha; a salaried worker is a pilgrim. Everyone works to be freed from poverty, ignorance, and anger, thereby attaining Nirvana. Therefore, if you want to know about Zen, study Japan's *sogo shosha*, or general trading companies.

This explanation tends to leave them much surprised because they are not aware that Zen and the "economic animal" stem from the same concept.

I suppose the above thoughts can be summarized by saying that worldly business is nothing more than the practice of religion, and by concentrating on it, you can reach Nirvana. This is substantiated by the fact that it is only the Japanese who are unhappy at the prospect of retirement. Americans look forward to it eagerly, even celebrating the event in a big way. In Japanese society, to "do nothing" is an expression of criticism, since no work means you are not practicing Buddhism. Such cultural differences between Japanese and Americans will not vanish overnight despite the criticisms.

With regard to the question of increasing Japanese arrogance, a public opinion poll was conducted jointly by *Yomiuri Shimbun* and Gallup to observe public opinion trends among major Western countries with the United States as the nucleus. The survey covered five countries, including European countries, and it found a gap in perception between Japan, the United States, and Europe.

In reply to the question: What will Japan be like in the twenty-first century (*see* Fig. 35), those that ranked Japan highly, saying that it will be an economic power ranking with the United States, stood at over 50 percent in the United States, 40 percent in the United Kingdom, and only 15 percent in Japan, in other words, the lowest of the five.

In reply to the question: Will it be difficult for Japan to maintain its present economic might, the affirmative response was twice as high in Japan as it was in the United States and France. In Japan, 28 percent of secondary school graduates and 44 percent of university graduates were pessimistic about the future of their country.

Fig. 35: THE JAPANESE ECONOMY IN THE 21st CENTURY

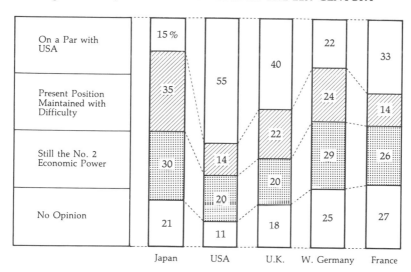

This lack of confidence in Japan by the Japanese, who are a well-educated people, surprised me. I remember that a lot of intellectuals in this country projected the decline of Japan in the early 1970s, when there was rampant environmental pollution and an oil crisis. Whenever times are difficult, the intellectuals subscribe to a pessimistic view of the future. Thus, intellectuals enjoy speaking ill of their country, which is hardly consistent with an arrogant race.

However, it is a sad fact that the trade friction is here to stay. In this connection, let me cite the opinion of Keiichi Konaga, former vice minister of International Trade and Industry, which is responsible for the nation's industrial policy. He claims that among Japanese products exported to the United States there are many items that are essential to America. Although a detailed survey remains to be made, Japanese exports to the United States include three types of items that are closely bound with the U.S. industry.

One item is exports by American companies operating in Japan, and a typical case is IBM Japan, which exports mainframes to its head office, or Texas Instruments Japan and Motorola Japan, which ship semiconductors to their head offices. These exports are valued at around $2 billion.

The second item is OEM (original equipment manufacturing) trade under American brand names. This type of export benefits American companies by expanding their product selection without any plant and equipment investment. For instance, Hitachi exports CPUs and mainframe peripherals to National Advanced Systems, while Fujitsu send magnetic storage devices to Memorex. Isuzu and Suzuki Motors export cars to General Motors and Mitsubishi Motors to Chrysler. These exports amount to $5 billion.

The third item includes parts and components exports that are indispensable to American manufacturing companies, such as parts for automobiles and communications equipment and semiconductors. These amount to an estimated $8 billion (the Japanese magazine, *Economist*, August 20, 1984).

Taken together, these exports amount to $15 billion, nearly half the Japanese trade balance surplus for 1984.

On the Japanese side, it is true that a number of obstacles exist, such as import testing and lengthy procedures. I will let Masaharu Gotoda, director-general of the Management and Coordination Agency that controls Japanese bureaucrats, speak here.

> Cosmetics are an example where it is utterly unnecessary to test them further in Japan. If they have been cleared in the United States, where the Caucasian race is said to have more sensitive skin, then further testing should be left to the consumers. The reason why the prime minister's call to buy more imports failed in 1985 was because former government officials are in organizations responsible for such testing. I can see how these people will look if testing of imports is

eliminated completely. Still, it is unreasonable of them to resist an issue of national importance. What is needed here is a relaxation of all restrictions.

It is a fact that these government officials exist, but however understandable their feelings are, it is they who will be responsible for the total isolation of Japan if the situation persists.

# 7

# Managerial Advice
# Based on Personal Experience

The foremost influence on the future of a business is the ability of its manager and employees. Various works on management techniques have been published, exhorting companies to adopt a culture, to give its employees a creative work environment, or to establish close contacts with its customers. Such suggestions are all excellent, but they have been heard too often, so I would like to offer some of my own advice based on a different perspective—my own experience.

EXPAND YOUR MAIN BUSINESS

First of all, no business should abandon its main line of work, as such a course almost inevitably brings disaster. Even Toyota Motor, one of Japan's top corporations, failed in its venture in mass-produced homes.

J. H. Peters, in his book *In Search of Excellence*, advocates this boldly, and the former chairman of Proctor & Gamble, Edward Harness, used to say that his company never departed from its base as it was not aiming to be a conglomerate. And with a few exceptions, most of the companies that have stuck to their main line of business have been rewarded with excellent records.

However, as mentioned in Chapter 1, this does not mean that

you have to stick to your main line of business in the narrow sense. If so, you will find yourself slowly but surely reaching the point of full growth, after which it is all downhill. What is important is to change the content of your business through innovation, and the way to do this is to expand on your main business while keeping to the same "tracks."

Take the case of 3M, for instance, a blue-chip company that deserves a place among the top ten companies in the United States. 3M has one basic product technology, which is painting and adhesives technology, and from this base it launched its innovation. 3M started out making sandpaper and magnetic tapes, then branched out into related fields with such new developments as sellotape, photosensitive paper, photographic film, traffic marker tape, agricultural tape (seeds for planting are put on rain-soluble tape), and surgical tape. In short, all its new products are centered around adhesive tape. It now has over 45,000 varieties of products, and its sales are well over ¥1 trillion.

Thus, the basis of any innovation policy is the development of new products by making use of the technology developed for the main business or by utilizing the same distribution channels as those of the main products.

In *The Life Expectancy of Corporations, Part II* (*Nihon Keizai Shimbun*, 1985), cases are cited to substantiate the fact that when a new business line accounts for over 70 percent of the main business, the company is on the road to decline because 70 percent of the business will be new. The book mentions successful case studies of companies that have changed the content of their business without changing their main line, such as Nippondenso—expanding from electrical equipment for autos to electronic products; Victor Co. of Japan—from audio products to laser discs; and Sharp—from household electrical appliances to electronic equipment.

The emphasis on expanding, instead of abandoning, the main line of business is not limited to technological companies. Ajinomoto, for example, started with food seasonings, and if it had stuck to these products it would have gone out of business long ago. However, seasonings account for only 10 percent of its sales today, with the remaining 90 percent coming from food-related products. Ajinomoto turns out close to one hundred different products, ranging from low-calorie artificial sweeteners to ready-made frozen pies to instant miso soup and coffee. Its merchandise makes use of the same distribution channels as Ajinomoto's food seasonings, showing how expertly the company coped while keep within the food distribution sector.

In cases of diversification into a completely unrelated business field, there are two formulas for success. The first is to make use of the experience of older employees. Today, with the rise in the average life expectancy of Japanese, management will be faced with the problem of having a lot of older employees, whose skills could be put into use in a subsidiary company, where they are given full freedom in managing it. The service sector would be best because this is where investment is minimal and where experience counts for a lot.

The second formula for successful diversification is the segregation of one department of a company to make it totally independent. For instance, a bank or a trading company could turn its computer division into a data processing company, or a steel producer could set up an independent engineering company. However, in view of the high failure rate that accompanies such ventures, the utmost care is necessary when planning such an undertaking.

Even large companies have not found this path easy. For example, after Sony had provided half the capital for a sporting goods import and distribution company called Sony Wilson, it suddenly pulled out in July 1986 and sold all its stock to Pepsi-Cola in the United States. Sony decided that the sporting goods business did not fit in with its image as an electric and electronics producer and withdrew from the business before it sustained any damage.

Similarly, Fujisawa Pharmaceutical went into the household

products market with a room deodorizer in 1978, only to withdraw in 1985, after coming to an agreement with Lion, the toothpaste and synthetic detergent manufacturer, on the sale of its household goods trading rights.

Such dynamic diversifications used to be in vogue in the United States, but the trend for conglomerates to revert to their main businesses has been striking. Exxon, one of the largest oil companies, entered the office machines field as a means of utilizing the huge profits it earned from the sudden price rise of crude oil. In 1986, however, it sold this new division to Olivetti of Italy in order to focus on its main business. RCA, too, disposed of a subsidiary in the insurance business in 1984 and sold its Hertz rent-a-car subsidiary in 1986.

## FIND A GENIUS FOR DEVELOPMENT

Judging from my own experiences in developing and exporting MT magnets, and in steering a think tank along the right tracks, I feel more and more that the key to new product development lies in the personality of the team leader, not the organization, and thus the right person must be found to take charge of development.

Such a person should also be able to work in total obscurity for a while, as product development is time-consuming and frustrating and results do not materialize overnight. (It took me five years for each of my projects—MT magnets and the think tank—and it was three years after I took charge of the magnetic steel division of Mitsubishi Steel before the company was back in the black.)

The project leader is the man that all the other workers watch as well as depend on, so he must possess the following three qualifications. First, he must have complete and utter devotion to the project at hand, showing unflagging enthusiasm and energy. Leaders such as Toshio Ikeda, the head of the independent computer development team at Fujitsu, Soichiro Honda, who made his company into one of world renown, and Kazuo Inamori, the "catalyst" of Kyocera—were all geniuses when it came to new product development.

The second qualification is that the leader must not lose confidence in himself in adverse situations. The management of 3M is comprised mostly of people who have found success after repeated failures. This reminds me of an anecdote I heard from a man who crossed the Arctic in a sleigh. He told me that if there is one dog in the pack that has run the distance before, all the other dogs will follow it.

The third qualification in a leader is his ability to persuade his team members, who all rely on him to motivate them in their work. Communication alone is not sufficient, and according to an experienced leader, "development" is just another word for "persuasive engineering."

There are others who will claim, with some truth, that the organization is more important than the team leader, but the problem of motivating the staff cannot be solved by an organization. An in-house project team or an independent in-house division for development may prove effective. If this is done, the leader must be given full control over his staff as well as his budget, with the provision of promotion for all the team members if the project is successful.

## DON'T STICK TO THE TOP SPOT

Such suggestions as a business should "create" ideas that lead to new product development, or a company should develop original technology, are both sound, but it is necessary to remember that not all blue-chip companies have been responsible for the development of the original technology they take advantage of. Many of them have succeeded in transforming the inventions of other companies into their own technological development.

IBM heads the list of *Fortune* magazines's blue-chip companies, and this company has been successful with its "watch and wait" policy to see how products of other countries and companies are faring on the market. Among the list of IBM products are many that were first "tested" by other companies and then adopted and sold by IBM. I have mentioned how Univac produced the world's first computer, a move that dealt a hard blow to IBM's accounting machines. However, using its technological skills to the utmost, IBM developed its own computer just after the Korean War had started in 1950 and computers were in great demand for military use. By making full use of its expert sales power, IBM overtook Univac without much effort.

Today the market share of minicomputers has declined due to the rise in the personal computer market, which was dominated by Apple Computer, its developer, for a long time. When IBM decided to enter this race after first observing market trends, it quickly wrenched the top spot from Apple.

In operational strategy, IBM is a lot like Matsushita Electric Industrial Co., whose entry into transistor radios, first developed by Sony, expanded that market rapidly. In VCRs, too, Matsushita was quick to adopt the VHS system that was developed by Victor of Japan, thereby winning the largest slice of that market. Both IBM and Matsushita seem comfortable in their positions just behind the front runner in their business strategy. It is perfectly fine to be placed first if your company is still growing, but remember that the potential for growth is ultimately more important.

Today, compact discs (CDs) are very popular with audio lovers. Years ago I remember asking Norio Ohga, Sony's president, which of his company's products would become popular in the future, and he named compact discs. In those days, even I had not heard much about that technology, and all it conjured up to me were shining silver discs. Now, of course, the advantages of CDs are obvious: undistorted sound, large storage capacity, and no damage through use.

However, the development of CD technology was riddled with problems, especially at a time when their future appeal was in some doubt. It was Philips that first developed CD technology, and Sony only joined Philips at a later stage. In 1984, when I dined with the person in charge of R&D at Philips, I was told that Philips has to use several Sony patents in the production of CDs.

## IBM and National Panasonic

The founders of Matsushita (National Panasonic) and IBM are very similar men in that neither Konosuke Matsushita nor Tom Watson, Sr., had the benefit of a complete education, proving the fallibility of the belief that only graduate engineers can manage high-tech companies. Second, both men were expert salesmen, Tom Watson demonstrating his skills even when he was still employed by NCR. When he left it to start IBM, he told his employees to build him new products and "I'll go out and sell them all."

Third, both men had a knack for winning people over. I heard at IBM Japan that when IBM had over ten thousand employees, Tom Watson knew them all by name. Moreover, he was familiar with the personal situation of his staff, often surprising an employee by saying, "Your son's starting grade school soon, isn't he?" Konosuke Matsushita is also known for his ingenious ways with people, with the result that all his employees are fascinated with Matsushita-ism.

Fourth, both Tom Watson and Konosuke Matsushita were financial wizards: Watson was an unrivaled financial manager, and Matsushita was a genius at accounting. Matsushita has a system of divisions that are financially independent, but all accounting is channeled through the head office accounting section. In this way, no factory division, say, can manipulate bookkeeping to make its performance look better than it actually is. If the division manager were responsible for accounts, he could ask his accountant to enter defective products as inventory in order to appear in better shape. A third party makes accounting more accurate in all respects.

Fifth, both Watson and Matsushita do not feel the need to be placed first, being satisfied with their positions as runner-up. Yet once a decision is made, they are quick to get into mass-production, thus securing the top position easily.

The steel industry, once Japan's key industry, is also in the runner-up position, as are Japanese automakers. Toyota was lagging far behind its American and European competitors before it began to overtake most of the world's front runners. The lesson that can be gleaned from these cases is that being in the top spot is irrelevant, for the first company to enter a new business field does not necessarily mean that it is an excellent company. Far more important is the ability to turn out reliable products, or win customers, enabling you at the same time to get a peep into the future of a market.

There are people, especially academics and critics, who are not involved in business and who do not like my advocation of the runner-up position. I do not mean to say that the first place is undesirable; to the contrary, if at all possible, creative, independent development of new technology is an excellent aim. However, in business management, it is often the case of selecting the best of several business techniques. (You would look rather silly if you told a company awash in red ink not to get overly concerned about being in the top spot. After all, profit is one way we evaluate a company's performance.)

This may seem to support criticism from some quarters that Japan should be more involved in creative, independent development of technology. In this instance I would like to ask the question: How would the world view Japan if it was to take the lead in creativity as well? It is better for all parties concerned if each maintains its advantage in its own field and specializes in it.

## LEARN FROM THE PAST

The characteristics of Japanese business management discussed so far only touch on the strong points, but there are a lot of weaknesses in it, too. *The Essence of Failure*, by Ryoichi Tobe et al. (Diamond Co., 1984), analyzes the reasons for Japan's defeat in World War II, and these reasons are applicable to business.

A comparison of the strategic and organizational natures of the Japanese and the American military clearly reveals the causes of Japan's failure. The first reason is vagueness of objective, illustrated by the Nomonhan Incident, in which the Japanese forces were decimated. It may surprise the reader to learn that no one, not even Imperial headquarters, knew why a skirmish started by the Japanese army in Manchuria should have led to this battle. And the Japanese soldiers at the front did not know why they were fighting either.

A similar lack of strategy characterized the naval battles off Leyte and in Midway. The Japanese have the tendency to be swept by feelings of "tacit understanding," or by a prevailing "atmosphere," and under the spell of such vague, indefinable feelings, will act without knowing why. This situation is often seen in the business sector.

The second reason for Japan's defeat is a cultural difference that results in disparate ways of thinking between Japanese and Americans. Japanese are good at inductive reasoning, reaching a goal by eliminating shared personal experiences, while Americans use deductive reasoning, which seeks a solution to individual problems through established rules. Thus, Americans are good at orchestrating grand projects, such as the World War II Manhattan Project for the development of atomic bombs and NASA's Apollo Program. Both projects are the result of detailed planning and crystal-clear objectives.

The Japanese army during the war was aware of the recklessness of the Imparl Operation but was carried away by General Mutaguchi's "conviction" of ultimate victory. It was equally impossible for the battleship *Yamato* to reach Okinawa when the enemy had air control; nevertheless, Deputy Chief of Naval General Staff, Jisaburo Ozawa, declared: "It is natural for the battleship to make a sally in the atmosphere prevailing at the time."

The third reason for Japan's defeat lies in the Japanese tendency to give priority to one type of technology at the expense of all others. No doubt the *Yamato* and the Zero fighter planes were both excellent pieces of machinery, but war is not fought with only battleships and Zero fighters but with a well-coordinated overall system comprising a logistics base, radio network, radar network, and so on. Japan concentrated on single components of the war effort at the expense of related technology and weapons system.

Americans, on the other hand, always start with a view of the whole, and then work to standardize each part of that whole. They make use of the entire system, not parts of it, and the result is a very solid information system today. Conversely, it can be inferred that Americans are not good at the manufacture of individual products.

The three weaknesses that resulted in Japan's defeat—vague strategy, inductive reasoning, unbalanced priorities—are also inherent in Japanese business management, which suffers from a very narrow view. Japan has to give serious thought to its weak points if it is to continue to be strong.

## THE BRIGHTER THE LAMP, THE DARKER THE SHADOW

High technology can be compared to a forceful blow of a hammer that has shattered our society, forcing many changes on it, and it must be remembered that not all the changes are necessarily advantageous. The negative effects are listed as follows.

**1. Employment.** With our sophisticated information technology, automation is rapidly moving from the factory into the office, taking away with it a number of jobs. The problem of redundant workers, which is a serious threat in the United States and Europe, is now being studied, with both the ILO (International Labour Organization) and the EC giving warnings about the rise in the number of workers affected by high technology. In Japan, however, labor unions are not so worried since unions are intracompany unions that reassign displaced workers to another part of the same company.

**2. A computer-controlled society.** Not so long ago, we could buy our railway tickets from the ticket window outside the railway station. Today tickets are sold by machines, which is all very well, but the machine cannot tell us where to change trains. In the office, a computer does the filing and makes statistical analyses for us, and this is said to free workers for more sophisticated jobs. But I can't help wondering if it's not a case of the computer controlling the employee.

**3. Violations of privacy.** With the growing use of computers that process and record all kinds of information, there is concern about possible violations of privacy in such personal areas as schooling, marital stability, family status, and annual income. The worst situation is the possibility of wrong information being fed into a computer, with the result that a person is misidentified for life. Once an information and communications network is built and improved, there is every likelihood of such occurrences. In addition, such a system is certain to find its way into important governmental or business offices, resulting in frequent leaks of secret information.

**4. Accidents.** When a communications system becomes more advanced and covers a wider sphere, a simple accident can have far-reaching consequences due to the scale of the system involved. A minor accident will result in extensive damage to such systems as banking or railways.

**5. The incompatibility of man and machines.** With progress in office automation, more computers and peripheral equipment will be used by office workers. Indeed businesses will begin and end with these machines, and in time they will invade the home. Man and machines are essentially incompatible, and it is not easy to live a life surrounded by machines without the attendant problems of stress. An allergy to machines will inevitably spread to people of all generations.

**6. A decline in mental faculties.** Japanese are good at mental calculation, but the pocket calculator will certainly have an affect on the mental faculties of schoolchildren today. A survey of high school teachers in the United States attempted to find out what problems, if any, were associated with the use of computers in classrooms. The results were divided equally between "problematic" and "no problem," indicating that there is no evaluation of the effect of computer use on education.

Technology is advancing at such a rapid pace that it is hard to keep up, let alone cope, with its negative factors. Thus it is good for businesses to remember the axiom: The brighter the lamp, the darker the shadow when dealing with applications of high technology.

## LOOK TEN YEARS AHEAD

One approach to innovation, in revitalizing a company, is in business management. I once had a talk with Takeshi Nagano, president of Mitsubishi Metal Corporation at a seminar sponsored by the Japan Productivity Center. His company used to be in serious financial trouble and withheld the payment of dividends to its shareholders for six years, but it has made a dramatic recovery in the past few years.

The reason for its turnabout, explained Nagano, was due entirely to its present chairman, former president, Yoshihiro Inai, who pushed ahead with plant and equipment investment in the midst of financial crises by looking ten years ahead into the future. In those days aluminum cans were not so widely used as they are today; yet he built seven production lines for these cans. Only one line was in operation initially, but today production is so brisk that more lines are needed. However, the move that really shocked the employees was Inai's acquisition of the deficit-ridden Nippon Silicon when his own company was producing a deficit of ¥1.5 billion. He was criticized both within and outside the company, but it was his foresight of the IC boom, as well as his decision to go ahead in difficult times, that resulted in Mitsubishi Metal's present strength in IC products.

I had a similar experience when I was in the magnetic materials division of Mitsubishi Steel. After the first oil crisis, I went ahead and ordered a Zundovidk ultraprecision multiple roll mill for building a pilot plant of powder metallurgical equipment for ferrites. To my chagrin, the plant was later discontinued and abandoned, and I still remember my frustration at the time. Management acted correctly when it decided to cut its losses then. Decisions concerning when to advance and when to retreat should be left to managers who are able to look ten years ahead into the future, and if they can see decline they can search for new roads leading to prosperity.

## THE "BE" GENERATION

In Chapter One, I coined the term the "be" generation to describe Japan's youth of today, who are totally different from members of my generation. Those of us of the prewar generation lived in circumstances bordering on poverty, bound by the moral obligation of self-sacrifice for the country, and our daily desire for food, clothing, and shelter, which were all in short supply. Our craving for these items outweighed all others. We were the "have" generation, and only those who have experienced those times, when the national income was one-twentieth its present level, can know what it was like.

The postwar generation born during the first baby boom reached maturity in the period of high economic growth in the 1960s, with their desire for food, clothing, and shelter fully satisfied. Their aim in life was to serve the company by working hard, so hard that they are now dubbed "workaholics." They also put all their energy into leisure and cultural activities, partaking in QC circles, cultural meetings, and overseas tours. They are the "do" generation.

The people of the "have" and "do" generations are characterized by strong loyalty to the company and an interest in self-advancement. They were the champions of Japanese business management as we know it today, represented by labor unions and lifetime employment, and they were the backbone of Japan's financial and economic success. By contrast, the values of our present generation seem to be altogether different. Here is an essay by Eiichiro Adachi, who won first prize in the 1985 Diamond Students Essay Contest. He wrote:

> We feel that promotion or advancement does not constitute the sole means of our self-expression in life. Rather, we wish to be involved in interesting work with frank and open-hearted friends. Members of the older generation think that because they are paid to do their job, hardship is a natural companion to work. Even if they found something interesting in their work, they would not qualify the work itself as interesting. . . . Movements aimed at discovering self-expression through work are gathering momentum in our generation. And we find nothing attractive in the Japanese way of business management.

From the above, it is apparent that these youngsters do not belong anywhere or to anything. Their only wish is to live at their own pace and discretion. For them, it is their occupation, not their company, that is at the center of their life. They find value in their difference from others. The fact that they show little concern for self-advancement is supported by a recent survey conducted by NHK. The older generation is dismayed that the young have no opposing concept, such as work *versus* pleasure. To them, statements like, "I'm crazy about surfing," and "I'm a copywriter," are the same.

The thinking of this generation, which is shaking itself free from a sole interest in work, is accepted by the young, although in varying degrees. In this are found the seeds of the future collapse of the Japanese way of business management.

How can the next generation of managers give the "be" generation something meaningful in work, thereby revitalizing business? This is an area that needs serious thought as well as serious reform. The hierarchical structure will have to be changed, independent venture businesses such as in-house and satellite businesses will have to be adopted, the seniority system will need to be abolished, and job mobility will have to be increased.

However, it remains to be seen whether the strength of Japanese corporations can be maintained when the new generation comes to play a dominant role in business. This is the task that Japanese industry has to tackle, now that we are stepping into the twenty-first century. The United States, too, has a number of tasks to face. What has become of the mighty United States of America? We hope that its frontier spirit will be rekindled and it will establish a new industrial image for the next century as America today stands poised between decline and prosperity.

# Index

cement industry, 14, 58, 100
ceramics, *see* new ceramics.
chemical industry, 42, 173
Chrysler, 154, 174, 180
Cii, 176
Club of Rome, 137
coal industry, 13, 14
communication procedures, 83
communications, 64, 65, 66, 96, 97, 101, 126, 127, 171; equipment, 25, 64, 150, 152; equipment, U.S. export of, 152, 180; machinery, 26; networks, 71, 83, 85, 131, 192; satellites, 90, 113, 125; systems, 83; technology, 151
compact discs, *Jee* CDs.
companies, life expectancy in Japan, 12, 14; life expectancy in U.S., 14
compatibility, of equipment, 85
computer industry, 133; manufacturers, 128; networks, 52; peripherals, 25, 95, 180; technology, 59, 171
computergraphics, 127
computerized production system, 55
computers, 19, 25, 41, 45, 52, 59, 60, 62, 68, 74, 76, 77, 80, 81, 82, 98, 104, 119, 128, 144, 153, 187, 192
consumer prices, 30; spending, 39; tastes, 48; needs, 48
contact lenses, 19
"convenience stores," 35
copying machines, 83, 96
cosmetics, 18, 180
Cray Research, 80
CSK, 38, 64

Dai Nippon Printing, 47, 48
Daiei, 35
Daikyo Kanko, 14
Daimler-Benz, 96
data communications, 83, 86

data processing, 71, 77, 119, 127, 184
databases, 81, 88, 97, 124, 131
DDX-P, 126
DEC, 80
declining industry, 48
defense expenditure, of Japan, 24; of U.S., 24
Delphi projection method, 61, 114, 137, 138
Deming, W. E., 141
Development Bank of Japan, 62
digital communications, 87
digital watches, 47, 122
distribution industry, 52, 53, 54; system, 51, 85, 124, 125
diversification, 55, 184, 185
"do" age/generation, 57, 114
Doi, 53
domestic market, of Japan, 27, 40, 122
Dow Jones, 88, 131
DRAM (dynamic random access memory), 74, 76, 153, 154

EC, 154, 191; *see also* Europe.
economic growth, 22; of Japan, 42
Economic Planning Agency, 65
economies of scale, 42, 43, 176
economy, of Japan, 15; of U.S., 150
Edison, Thomas, 169–70
Edo, Hideo, 16
electrical machinery, 64
electronic appliances, 96
electronic technology, 66–71
electronics, 44, 61, 64, 70, 96, 97, 117, 146, 160; equipment, 65; industry, 70; technology, 61
employment, stability of, 22
Energy and Resources Subcommittee (Science and Technology Agency), 114
energy conservation, 137

Epson, 77
equipment standardization, 85
Esaki, Reona, 78, 168
Esso, 14
Europe, 41, 42, 43, 66, 159, 166, 168, 178; see also EC.
exchange rate, yen–dollar, 27, 29, 150
expenses, private, 50
"expert system," 129
exports, of Japan, 23, 24, 25, 28, 30, 39, 146, 157
Exxon, 185

facsimiles, 18, 83, 86
factory management technology, 61
FAME (forecast and appraisals for management evaluation), 61, 144
Familia model, 56
Fanuc, 77
Fanucman, 97–98
farmers cooperatives, 123
Federation of Specialty Stores Association, 16
ferrites, 17, 100
fertilizer industry, 14
fifth-generation computer, 81, 82, 134
finance, 124
Florida, 88
FMS (flexible manufacturing systems), 55, 98, 99
Ford, 154
Fortune, 186
France, 23, 25, 36, 43, 87, 88, 89, 146, 176, 178
fuel cells, 44
Fujisawa Pharmaceutical, 184
Fujitsu, 20, 76, 80, 127, 176, 180, 185
functional materials, see materials, functional.
functional polymers, 44, 100

furniture, 53
Furukawa, 13

Gallup, 178
GATT (General Agreement on Tariffs and Trade), 154
GDP (gross domestic product), 36–37
Gell-Mann Research Institute, 42
gene recombination, 44, 60, 108
General Motors, 132, 154, 180
GNP, of Japan, 15, 27, 29, 30, 36, 106; of United States, 29; of Switzerland, 29
Golf model, 55
Gotoda, Masaharu, 180
graying society, 31
growth rate, 29
Grundrich, 25
GTE Telenet, 126

Hakodate Dockyard, 50
Hanover, 70, 95, 99
hardware, 59, 61, 64, 71, 74, 119–21
hardware market, in the U.S., 127
Harley-Davidson, 27
Harness, Edward, 182
"have" age/generation, 57, 194
health insurance contributions, 36
HEMT (high-electron mobility transistor), 79, 104
high technology, 25, 41, 44, 45, 62, 64, 65, 66, 96, 116, 117, 123, 175
high-tech industry, 64, 116, 117, 120; of U.S., 151, 154
high-tech investments, 62, 64
Hiroshima, 56
Hitachi, 72, 180
Hitachi Maxell, 13
Hokkaido, 87
"hollowing out," of American industries, 150

home banking, 88
Honda, Soichiro, 185
Honda Motor, 27, 169, 170
household appliances, 33, 59, 183
housewives, 32–36, 57
housing industry, 16, 18
housing starts, in Japan, 16, 70
Hoya, 54

Iacocca, Lee, 116
IBM, 80, 126, 129, 153, 176, 180, 186-87, 188
Ibuka, Masaru, 144
IC industry, in Japan, 166; manufacture, 73, 77, 120; production, 79–80; technology, 59, 60, 77, 78
ICs (integrated circuits), 18, 59, 66, 68, 70, 71, 72, 73, 74, 75, 76, 78, 79, 99, 117, 120, 122, 122, 132, 153, 154, 193
Ikeda, Toshio, 185
ILO (International Labour Organization), 191
import restrictions, of Japan, 26
imported technologies, 41
imports, 26; from U.S., 149; of Japan, 25, 146, 157; of other countries, 25
IN (information network), 126
Inai, Yoshihiro, 193
Inamori, Kazuo, 104, 185
Indiana Steel Corp., 168
industrial engineering, 66
industrial pollution, 43
industry, of Japan, 42
information, 64, 65, 66, 101
information age, 117; industry, 127; management, 52; processing, 56, 128; sector, 22; society, 18–22, 59, 81, 82, 85, 117, 134, 136, 151; technology, 191
Inmalsat, 113
innovation, 46, 183; see also organ-

izational innovation; product innovation.
INS (information network systems), 60, 71, 86-87, 97
Institute of Space and Astronautical Science, 112
Intec, 64, 126
Intel, 68
intellectual technology, 61, 136–38
Intelsat, 113
interest rates, 27
International Society of Materials, 154
internationalization, 22–30
investment, in high technology, 62, 64; in plant and equipment, 38, 39, 40, 180; in public works, 38; in manufacturing, 62, investment trends, 62
ISDN (integrated services digital network), 86
Ishikawajima-Harima Heavy Industries, 170
ISSCC (International Solid-State Circuit Conference), 159
Isuzu, 180
Ito, Masatoshi, 35
Ito, Yoshikazu, 19
Ito-Yokado, 35, 46

Japan, foreign misunderstanding of, 177; confidence in, 179
Japan Air Lines, 13
Japan Industrial Standard (JIS), 168
Japanese National Railways (JNR), 38, 51, 103; freight division of, 51
Japan Productivity Center, 193
Japan Tobacco Inc., 38
Joban Tanko, 13
"just-in-time" systems, 45, 61, 138–39, 174, 176

Kadota, Yasuhiro, 139

robots, 18, 19, 44, 56, 60, 77, 78, 97–98, 117, 175
rockets, 41
Royal, 13

Saito, Eishiro, 12
Sakaiya, Taichi, 13
*Sankei Shimbun*, 164
Sasebo, 49
Sasebo Heavy Industries, 49
Satellite Business Systems, 91
satellite communications, 60, 87, 91
savings, 37, 39, 40
Schumpeter, Professor Joseph, 46
Science and Technology Agency, 78, 104, 114
Secom, 13, 47
Securities Patrol Agency, 38
Seiko, 59, 122
Seino Transportation, 53
Sejima, Ryuzo, 36
Sekisui House, 16
semiconductor industry, in Japan, 153–55; in U.S., 153–55
semiconductor market, 74; substrates, 47; technology, 79, 153; trade, 153
Semiconductor Research Institute, 165
semiconductors, 25, 78, 79, 103, 105, 154, 165, 180
senior citizens, 31
service industry/sector, 38, 45, 52, 56–58, 123, 124, 127, 184
Seven-Eleven Japan, 35
sewing machines, 74
Sharp, 47, 75, 77, 183
Shewhart, W. E., 140
Shinkansen "bullet" train, 51, 73, 97
shipbuilding industry, 14, 49, 122, 156
Shockley, William, 157, 166, 168, 170

Siemens, 25, 176
Sigma Project, 134
Silicon Island (Kyushu), 73
Silicon Valley (California), 73
Skylark, 14
Small and Medium-sized Enterprises Agency, 120
social security payments, 36
Softnomics Center, 32
software, 20, 22, 56, 59, 60–61, 64, 66, 71, 73, 74, 78, 79, 80, 82, 83, 97, 119–21; applications of, 122–26; crises of, 132–35, 153, 171; development of, 81, 127–129; sales of, 119; standards, improvements in, 129–32
software industry, 128; in Japan, 127, 128; in U.S., 127, 128
software market, 127; in Japan, 128; in U.S., 127
solar power, 112, 113
solid-state circuits, 160
Sony, 18, 47, 144, 157, 166, 169, 170, 171, 184, 187
Sord, 80
South Korea, 155–56
Soviet Union, 161
space development, 113
space shuttles, 44
space technology, 60, 107, 112–13
Special Advisory Committee on Administrative Reform, 36
SRAM (static random access memory), 74
standards and certifications system, of Japan, 146
Star Wars, *see* U.S. Strategic Defense Initiative.
statistical quality control, 140–41
steel, 17, 100, 101, 106, 156, 157; industry, 42, 70, 117, 122, 155–56, 173, 189; manufacturers, 43, 58; mills, 42

Umesao, Tadao, 19
underwear, 32
unemployment, in U.S., 22
unemployment rates, 29
United Kingdom, 24, 43, 44, 87, 88, 89, 165, 166, 178
United States, 14, 21, 22, 23, 24, 25, 26, 27, 33, 40, 43, 44, 45, 59, 62, 66, 71, 72, 79, 80, 87, 87, 88, 89, 91, 92, 96, 99, 113, 116, 126, 128, 129, 131, 132, 137, 141, 144, 145, 146, 151, 153, 154, 155, 159, 168, 171, 173, 175, 176, 178, 179, 183, 185, 191, 196, 198
Univac, 68, 187
U.S. Corp., 156
U.S. Department of Commerce, 24, 62
U.S. Federal Reserve Board, 40
U.S. Strategic Defense Initiative (Star Wars), 96, 113
U.S. Trade Act (1974), 154

vacuum tubes, 68, 72, 75, 77
VAN (value-added network), 52, 53, 107, 125-26
VCRs, 18, 47, 59, 74, 150, 187
venture businesses/companies, 64, 79-80, 177
Victor, 183, 187
video cassettes, 91
video discs, 71, 91, 92, 94
Video Shack, 92
videotex, 87-89, 97, 123; consumer acceptance of, 88
Videotron, 88
VLSIs (very large-scale integrated circuits), 44, 68, 72, 73, 74, 78
Volcker, Paul, 40
Volkswagen, 55

Wacoal, 32, 47

watches, 47, 53, 59, 74, 78, 96, 117, 122
Watson, Tom, Sr., 188
weather satellites, 113
Webb, Dr. James E., 136
welfare system, 36
West Germany, 23, 25, 33, 36, 43, 44, 70, 87, 146, 161, 176
Westinghouse, 155
White Paper on Science and Technology (1984), 157; on Small and Medium-sized Enterprises (1985), 61; on Trade (1984), 124
"window-seat tribe," 31
women, 54; changing role of in Japan, 32-35; educational level of in Japan, 33; educational level of in U.S., 33; educational level of in West Germany, 33; see also housewives.
workers, 21; blue-collar, 22; gold-collar, 22; white-collar, 22
World War II, 41, 66, 190

Yakult, 47
Yamamoto, Shichihei, 177
Yamanashi, 78
Yamasaki, Yoshiki, 56
Yamato Transport, 46, 52
Yamazaki Ironworks, 99
Yawata Steel, 43
yen, value of, 30; see also exchange rate.
Yodobashi Camera, 53
*Yomiuri Shimbun*, 178
Yoshino Hiroyuki, 27
Yukawa, Hideki, 19

Zen, 177-78

定価2,900円
in Japan

財団
法人 **国際文化フォーラム**
# THE JAPAN FORUM

〒163-0726　東京都新宿区西新宿2-7-1
新宿第一生命ビル26階
Shinjuku Dai-ichi Seimei Bldg. 26F
2-7-1 Nishishinjuku, Shinjuku-ku, Tokyo 163-0726
Phone: 03-5322-5211  Fax: 03-5322-5215
E-mail: forum@tjf.or.jp  http://www.tjf.or.jp/